ANNABELLE

AND THE GREAT HURRICANE

BY

EVELYN GILL HILTON

BASED ON THE TRUE STORY OF THE DEADLIEST HURRICANE EVER TO HIT AMERICA AND OF A FRONTIER FAMILY CAUGHT IN IT.

First published by Dog Ear Publishing
4010 W. 86th Street, Ste H
Indianapolis, IN 46268
www.dogearpublishing.net

ISBN: 978-160844-838-8

This book is printed on acid-free paper.

Printed in the United States of America

Illustrations by Evelyn Gill Hilton with some by Dover Illustrations

I want to dedicate this book to my sister,
Susan Gill Radle.

Thank you for helping me tell the story of our ancestors, Susie.
Like me, salt water runs through your veins
and the love of the seas is in your heart!
Love,
Big Sis Evelyn

TABLE OF CONTENTS

Chapter

Historical Map of the Eastern United States

Texas Coastal Map During the 1800's

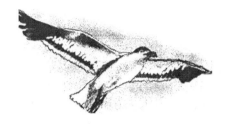

CHAPTER 1:

Last Summer Vacation

Dear Reader,

Hello, my name is Annabelle. I am a very old, porcelain doll. Long ago, in 1871, I was created by a well-known doll maker who lived in Germany, a country in Europe. Then, I was sent, along with twenty-three other dolls, to a dressmaker in the nearby country of France to be outfitted with an expensive set of clothes and, from there, we were shipped across the Atlantic Ocean in a large, wooden sailing ship to Galveston, Texas, in America.

A porcelain doll was quite costly in those days and highly prized by the lucky girl who received such a treasure. I was purchased in the Galveston seaport for my very first owner, a young girl named Laura Tilton. I adored Laura and thought we would be happy forever, but I sadly learned that humans grow up as Laura eventually did, leaving me behind. She married and later gave me to her youngest daughter, Effie, who loved me very much. However, I did not think that I could ever love another little girl again, only to be forgotten when my new owner grew up.

This is the story of my life and how I learned to love again during the 'Great Galveston Hurricane of 1900'. It is based on true events surrounding that monster storm. I was trapped, along with Laura, Effie and other family members, on Galveston Island during the most frightening night of our lives. This is also the story of my frontier family's unflinching faith and courageous struggle to survive the 'Deadliest Hurricane to Ever Hit America'.

I hope you find this book intriguing and exciting, but most of all, an inspiration to you during your own times of struggle.

Yours very truly, Annabelle

September 5, 1900~~The Cove, Three Days Before the Hurricane

It was early Thursday morning and the old rooster, Sparky, was crowing to signal the first light of day peeping over the horizon. Because school was out for the long summer break and the rice harvest, Laura and Fielden Stubbs' children were still asleep. In those early Texas days, frontier children were needed to help with the important work of planting and harvesting crops, so school was in session only from late September until early May. Since the little, one-room school house in The Cove community wouldn't open for the fall session for another two weeks, Laura talked with her husband about going to Galveston for a last summer visit.

Laura's sister-in-law, Henrietta, had sent word with her husband, Benjamin, that she would share the ripe pears and figs in her backyard if Laura would come and help her can the late fruit and make fig preserves. She also had Ben tell his sister to bring her new treadle sewing machine (a recent popular invention that every woman was clamoring for) so they could make the children some new school clothes. Ben would take us back to Galveston with him and I knew that Laura's youngest daughter, little Effie, my newest owner, would take me with her. I loved my very first home in America more than any other place, so I was elated! Fielden readily agreed to the trip, so it was settled. Laura and their three youngest children would sail back to the island with Ben on his big, wooden schooner.

Since it was harvest season, their two older boys, Martin and Wilbur, were staying home to help Fielden do the heavy field work of cutting rice and loading it into large tow sacks, then hauling it by wagon to Grandmother Annie's big, backyard pier. Laura's older brother would then load it onto his schooner on his twice-weekly river run to The Cove and take it to the Galveston Seaport to sell.

Laura's mother, Annie, and Annie's oldest son, Ben, owned the nearby boat loading dock, which was officially named *Tilton's Transport Enterprises*. However, everyone just called it the *Old River Dock*, since it was on the river that flowed right through The Cove community. Grandmother Annie and Grandpa Charles, as all the children called them, had earned their living for many years with this boat hauling business but, after he had grown too old to sail to the Galveston Seaport and back, Ben had taken over that part of the business. Since they lived nearby, Grandmother Annie often had the help of Laura's older daughters, Flavia and Bessie, in overseeing the farmers' goods that were brought to the pier. Ben sailed the schooner back and forth between Galveston and Old River Dock once or twice a week to pick up the produce. Every now and then, he even ferried passengers to the island.

The Cove's fertile land and frequent rains yielded farmers and ranchers, who were willing to work hard, excellent crops and lush green grass for their cattle, but getting them to the seaport was very difficult. Cattle had to be driven for many miles around the coast to the only bridge that connected Galveston to the mainland near Houston. Ben's schooner, *Black Jack II*, provided the perfect solution for farmers on the rivers.

But, back to my exciting news—I wanted to shout from the kitchen table to my current owner, little Effie Pearl, that we were going to Galveston. To my sorrow, my previous owner, Laura, had grown up and married her sweetheart, Fielden. He had built a wonderful house for them on acreage from Laura's mother and they had made it a loving home with seven children over the years. I now belonged to Effie because she loved dolls but I could not return that love because I knew that she, too, would one day grow up. This made my heart sad and I was glad that she did not know.

Charles and Annie Tilton's Home and Old River Dock

Benjamin, and his wife, Henrietta, owned a large, three-story home near his pier on the Galveston Island wharf, where he worked when he was not sailing across Galveston Bay to pick up produce from the coastal farms along the Trinity and Old Rivers. Ships from many countries in the world came into Galveston Bay and many docked a ways out from the piers. They could be sailed into Galveston Bay at high tide but were too large to dock in the shallow water near the wharf.

In the early days, Charles Tilton and his son, Ben, and then, in later years, Ben Tilton and his son, Daniel, would take a rowboat out to the ship and negotiate with the captain for the best price to unload their goods. Ben Tilton and his men were known by ship captains to have fair prices and to handle their goods quickly and carefully. The ship captains, in turn, would buy goods and produce from the farmers through Ben. His father and he had built up good business reputations because they were known to be honest.

When Effie and Daisy got up that morning and learned the news, they squealed in delight and danced about in excitement because they loved going to Uncle Ben and Aunt Henrietta's big home near the beach. Since their cousins were also going to be there for a visit, they were very excited. Henrietta's daughter, Rachel, was coming home and bringing her two children, Glenn and Janie. They were close in ages to Effie and Daisy and were great fun!

"Take Annabelle to your bedroom, Effie, and give little Donnie his breakfast for me, please." Laura said with a smile before she turned back to the wood stove to stir the oatmeal. Effie nodded obediently, running to her room with me hanging under her arm.

Their older sisters, except for Ola who was grown and married, Flavia and Bessie, were off visiting cousins, so only Laura, her two youngest daughters and three year-old son, Don, would be accompanying Benjamin back. Effie and Daisy's big brothers, fifteen year-old Martin and thirteen year-old Wilbur, planned to stay home to help their father work.

Daisy and Effie Dancing

Like free-spirited Laura, all of her children loved the cool Gulf of Mexico water and Galveston Island's warm, sandy beach. Although she and her dear Fielden had seven children now, with two of them almost grown, I knew that she felt like a young girl again at the thought of going to Galveston. She felt a bit sad, though, about leaving the two boys at home, so she walked outside to talk to them.

"Boys, breakfast is ready. I've been thinking that you might want go with us to Galveston tomorrow. You like the beach and sailing on Uncle Ben's schooner." Laura smiled as she reminded tall, lanky Martin and his perky young brother of these facts.

Their chores finished, the two boys followed her back into the house for breakfast. After washing up on the back porch, they hurriedly pulled chairs up to the kitchen table and looked hungrily over the food.

Martin and His Younger Brother, Wilbur

"Uh, we'd rather stay here with Pa and help him. He's got a lot of work to do, Ma. We'll be out in the fields from sun-up till dark every day harvesting rice." Martin and Wilbur both looked at each other and then their plates, nodding seriously. The boys' unusually helpful attitude caught Laura's attention as they continued to explain.

"Yeah, Ma, besides, who wants to can fruit and sew clothes like a girl when Pa needs our muscles so bad?" piped up younger, brown-haired Wilbur. Laura chuckled to herself at the thought of her boys in aprons sloshing fruit all over Henrietta's kitchen floor. Their reasons continued to flow freely while she listened with interest.

Then, without thinking, Wilbur suddenly let the cat out of the bag. "Thanks anyway, Ma, but Pa's counting on us to mow the playing field tomorrow, too, for the big base—Ouch!" Wilbur let out a muffled cry of pain as Martin gave his shin a well-aimed kick beneath the table. "Now, why'd you go and do that?" He yelled at Martin before realizing that he had just given away the big secret!

"Dumbbell!" His big brother, Martin, whispered through his teeth and glared at Wilbur, who suddenly realized the error he had just made. Then, both boys jumped up and flew out of the house before their mother could scold them for name-calling or learn the rest of their plans. But now, The Cove men's big recreation secret was out!

That evening, Fielden promised Laura that he and the two boys would stop by to see her mother, known to everyone as 'Grandmother Annie,' in the morning on their way to the fields and also to let Ben know that he would have three passengers going back with Dan and him to Galveston Island.

"Oh, and don't forget to remind her about the men's big baseball game," Laura mentioned. Her eyes twinkled as she continued to sweep the kitchen floor. Fielden stopped and looked back, then left the room grinning and shaking his head. He never could put anything over on his smart Laura.

September 6~~The Cove, Two Days Before the Hurricane

Friday morning, I heard Laura rise before dawn, while everyone else was still sleeping. I knew her familiar habits, from years gone by, as she dressed and pulled her long, black hair into a bun at the back of her head, sticking metal hairpins in to hold it in place. Then, she slipped quietly out of the bedroom and walked through the kitchen, onto the back porch and out into the backyard. I knew that she was pouring a pitcher of water down into the pump to prime it and then was pumping water up from the well. The screen door shut behind her, as she brought a bucket of cool water in, set it on the back porch shelf and poured some into a basin to wash her face and hands. Then, I heard the kitchen's big, iron stove door open and the sound of wood being loaded in for a fire.

The icebox door squeaked and I knew she was taking out the two chickens and cookie dough she had fixed the evening before. Soon the aroma of frying chicken, coffee and buttermilk biscuits filled the house along with big, thick sugar cookies that the family lovingly called 'tea-cakes'. It wasn't long before I heard little Donnie repeating "Mama, mama," and banging a spoon on his highchair.

It wasn't long before Fielden entered the kitchen and gave his wife a big hug. "My, you're a busy little bee this morning." He picked up Donnie and swung him in the air. "What smells so good, Laura?" He sat the laughing, little boy down, poured himself a steaming cup of coffee, and sat down at the long oak table, which sat in the middle of the big kitchen, to enjoy it.

"I will not go off and leave my men harvesting the rice and working cattle all day without some supper," Laura replied coyly. "Besides, the girls and Donnie will need lunch today on the boat." Fielden adored his thoughtful Laura and she loved her dear, funny husband. "Here is a cookie for you, Donnie, and one for your Papa," Laura smiled and handed each of them a warm teacake, as she put the second sheet of dough balls into the oven. Soon Laura went into the girls' bedroom and packed their clothes in the early morning light. She roused Effie and Daisy, with me tucked between them in their big feather bed, from their sound sleep. Tall Daisy favored Fielden with dark brown hair, tan skin and pretty, gray eyes, while little Effie looked much like Laura with coal black hair, light skin and pretty sea-green eyes. They groggily rubbed their eyes but, as soon as they remembered the adventure that lay ahead,

The Girls Asleep

they jumped up, pulled on their petticoats, dresses and high top shoes as quick as they could, giggling and chattering all the while!

*****

After a hurried breakfast, Fielden hitched the horses up to the wagon and loaded in his girls and their baggage. He looked at little Don, Daisy and Effie. "Girls, help your mother take care of Donnie. Effie, are you sure you want to take your porcelain doll?"

Little Effie nodded seriously and pulled me close as she settled into the back of the big wagon. "Annabelle likes to go to Galveston, too, Pa," she assured him, nodding hardily.

Fielden lightly patted my head. "All right Annabelle, I'm depending on you to take good care of our Effie, Daisy and little Don."

The family would remember his prophetic words long after the vacation. Laura smiled and looked at her youngest daughter and me for a moment, and I was sure she was thinking of the time long ago when she had carried me everywhere she went. Children's toys were rare in those days and a porcelain doll was an especially cherished possession.

We set off at a fast clip for the two-mile ride to Grandmother Annie's house beside the Old River dock built by her husband, Charles, many years ago. She still made a living from her farm and by charging six cents for each sack of the rice or cotton and four cents a bushel for vegetables that Cove farmers shipped to the Galveston seaport. Thus, the Tilton family was able to make a living and help their friends, as well.

It wasn't long before we arrived at Grandmother Annie's house and spotted the mast and American flag of Ben's schooner out in the river. Ben's grown son, Daniel, hopped onto the pier and waved to us. The children ran up to their grandmother's house to announce our arrival and she opened the screen door, calling everyone in for coffee. The old lady, mother of nine children, never tired of having her house filled with family.

Ben and Daniel Unloading the Schooner

Her strong, rugged face beamed with pleasure to have her oldest son, Ben, her grandson, Daniel, her youngest daughter, Laura, and her son-in-law, Fielden, as well as her grandchildren all together, sitting around her big, oak kitchen table.

After a short visit, Ben decided that they needed to get under way for the three-hour trip. A ship filled with bananas all the way from Mexico was docked beside his wharf in the Galveston harbor and he and Daniel needed to be there to oversee the unloading. He assured his mother he would sail back the very next day to pick up the last of the season's harvested rice. Ships were waiting in the harbor now to buy it and take it to far-away ports.

Grandmother Annie waved good-bye while Fielden hugged Laura and his children and urged them to have a safe trip. Then, they boarded the schooner, *Black Jack II*, which had been named by Grandfather Charles, who had once been a pirate with Jean Lafitte. Daniel untied the heavy rope from the dock and coiled it up on the boat deck while Ben raised the sails and took the wheel. There was a fair wind blowing, filling out the sails, so I knew we would make good time down the rivers and across the bay.

"Henrietta will be so glad to have you and the children, Laura." Ben remarked. "We don't see enough of you these days. Rachel and her two children have come over from Houston on the new wooden bridge, so you all can catch up on the latest gossip!" He laughed out loud.

Laura grinned in delight and Effie and Daisy clapped and squealed. They would all be glad to see Ben and Henrietta's daughter, Rachel, and cousins, Glen and Janie. It had been since last Christmas. Excitement reigned as Ben steered his boat out into the smooth Old River's downstream current that lead into the larger Trinity River and then out into the Galveston Bay.

CHAPTER 2:

Story Telling Time on the Boat

Soon into the trip, Ben noticed that the girls were acting peculiar. They couldn't sit still and kept looking at each other as though they had a secret. Finally, Laura laid little Donnie, who'd been sleeping in her arms, down and signaled them with a nod of her head.

"Uncle Ben, Dan!" Daisy jumped up. "We have a true story to tell you!" In the days before radios and televisions, stories were always regarded as prized entertainment and great fun. The girls were in their element, so Effie handed me to her mother and cleared her throat for her big moment.

Ben glanced at Dan, questioningly. Daniel shrugged his shoulders and shook his head. They wondered what on earth the girls had cooked up for their entertainment this trip.

"This is a very good story that really happened last week, so you have to listen to what I say carefully," said Effie seriously. Ben and Daniel nodded.

Effie began telling the story while Daisy, the dramatic actress of the family, made it even better by acting out each scene. Effie pulled herself up as tall as possible and began to speak slowly and loudly in her most animated and mysterious voice:

"One morning, Mama was in the kitchen all alone while we were at school and Papa was out in the rice field. The back porch door was open because it was so hot. Suddenly, she heard the water bucket and drinking dipper fall off the back porch shelf, so she turned around to see what had caused the accident. There, in the doorway, stood a huge brown cougar! The color drained out of Mama's face but she stood very still and the cougar did, too. His mean, yellow eyes were locked on hers. Mama's head began to spin and she thought she would faint, but she reminded herself that a Texas frontier woman and a Tilton, to boot, must be brave and strong for her family. She prayed a very short, silent prayer, asking the Lord to help her, and she suddenly reckoned that perhaps the big cat was confused about where he was, like once when a chicken flew through the open door and didn't know how to get back outside. Sooo, she yelled loud and shook the tail of her apron at him to shoo him outside."

Cougar in Kitchen

Daisy grabbed her long skirts like an apron and shook them, all the while, hollering at the top of her lungs, *"Go On! Get Out of My House, You Mangy Ole Cougar, Get Out!"*

Seeing that they had Ben and Daniel's full attention now, the girls continued their dramatic performance with even more enthusiasm.

Effie continued, *"It didn't do a bit of good though. He just kept standing there, breathing hard and growling and staring at her. Mama knew that, at any moment, he would pounce on her, so she had to do something quickly. She slowly picked up a dish from the sink and threw it at him, but it smashed against the wall in back of him. The crash distracted the cougar for just an instant and he turned to look behind him. When he did, Mama saw her chance. She ran as fast as her legs would carry her into the parlor and slammed the door behind her. Just as it slammed shut, she heard the animal's big body crash against it, almost breaking it!"*

Daisy complied by twirling around and slamming herself into the helm and into Uncle Ben, who stood beside it, steering the boat.

"Mama ran over and grabbed Papa's shotgun and shells down from the fireplace mantle and loaded it. 'I'm not about to be your supper today!' She mumbled under her breath. Then, she slowly cracked the door to the kitchen and looked for the animal. Now, he was standing on the kitchen table, growling and mad as could be! He spotted her, squinted his wild, yellow eyes and bared his big, sharp teeth. Then, he screamed that horrible scream that sounds like a baby and crouched down to leap onto his prey, which was Mama."

Daisy crouched down and made the appropriate cougar noises.

"But Mama stood her ground and shouted, 'And you get off my kitchen table!' She aimed the gun at his head and squeezed the trigger slowly with her finger."

Daisy pantomimed the action and yelled, *"Boom!"* as loudly as she could. By this time, Ben and Daniel's eyes were round and their mouths were hanging wide open!

"She hit him, but that old cougar stood like he was frozen for several seconds just looking at her, then he tumbled down onto the floor, as dead as a doornail!" Mama had hit him right between the eyes, then, she dragged him out of the house by his hind legs."

Daisy now became the cougar and tumbled down onto the deck. She lay very still, holding her throat and hanging her tongue out. Both

Ben and Daniel stood riveted in amazement. Effie and Daisy stood up together and gave their audience their best curtsy, signaling that their story was all finished. The audience clapped enthusiastically!

"Well, that's about the finest story I believe I've ever heard. You will have to tell it again when we get home," Daniel said. He and Ben nodded their heads and applauded the grinning girls again.

"Did you really do that?" Daniel finally asked Laura when he caught his breath. They looked from Laura to the girls and back to Laura again in disbelief.

Laura nodded and said in a practical voice. "I did what had to be done." She blushed, then smiled with an air of pride. "And later that evening, Fielden buried that old cougar out in the woods."

"Look, we have the proof!" Effie ran over to the Singer sewing machine Laura had brought with her to sew new school clothes. She dramatically pulled off the canvas cover and pointed to the machine. There on the top were three deep claw marks where the cougar had scratched it when he leaped up onto the table.

"I always thought you were brave, Laura," bragged Ben. "Now, I know it for sure!"

"Well, I *am* the daughter of a pirate," Laura answered and every-one laughed.

"A Privateer," Ben smiled and corrected her. "And a brave daughter, too." Ben said, still shaking his head.

"And you are the son of a privateer too, Uncle Ben! That makes Dan, Effie, Donnie and me the grandchildren of a privateer," Daisy exclaimed. Ben nodded as the girls chattered excitedly to him and Daniel during the rest of the boat ride, hardly giving them time to think of answers.

The entire Tilton family knew well the difference between a pirate and a privateer, due to Ben's and Mother Annie's frequent tales about Ben's father. Father Charles had been kidnapped from a whaler when he was only a boy by some cutthroat pirates who took him to Jean Lafitte's base camp on Galveston Island, just off the Texas coast. He was offered a job aboard Lafitte's ship and liked the sea-faring life so much that he stayed with the buccaneers for six years.

Lafitte, a famous privateer and his men, had helped the American government defeat the British during the 1812 Battle of New Orleans, when England attacked our country for the last time. He was hailed as a national hero and, afterward, he had been hired by President Madison, as a privateer, to rid America's waters of the fierce Spanish Galleons threatening our coast. In return, he and his men were allowed to keep the galleons' treasures, which had been plundered from Mexico and were being taken back to Spain.

"Uncle Ben, see my doll, Annabelle!" Effie cried, waving me around in front of him.

"Well, I'll be a hogtied river rat!" said Ben in mock seriousness. He winked at Dan and Laura. "This looks like the same porcelain doll I bought for your mama years ago when she was just a young girl. I still remember Dan digging that doll out of a crate that had come all the way from Germany. It looks like she has a new blue dress."

"Mama made it for her when she gave Annabelle to me," replied Effie. "I have to be very careful and not get her dirty."

Ben smiled and his eyes twinkled as he cast another glance at his little sister, Laura. Then he reminisced, telling of the long-ago time when she was a young girl, as though it were yesterday. Daisy and Effie sat riveted, listening to Uncle Ben talk about their mother's childhood.

He filled his corncob pipe and lit it, then began in his slow, southern drawl:

"Girls, your mother, Laura, was just about eight years old when she first learned to jump from the crow's nest high up on the mast of our Father Charles' sunken pirate ship in Lost Lake. Mother Annie walked down to the lake to check on us kids. All of us boys were swimming while Old Rastus, an old ex-slave and now the family's trusted hired-hand and friend, sat nearby watching.

Suddenly, Mama spotted little Laura high up in the schooner's crow's nest. "Look, look at me, Mama!" Laura waved, shockingly standing there in her long, white pantaloons and camisole top (a cotton undergarment for girls, similar to a boy's undershirt) at the top of the mast, which stuck up into the air about twenty-five feet above the water. Like her brothers, she had shinnied up the rickety wood ladder nailed to the mast to get to the lookout bucket. Suddenly, she jumped down into the dark water while we all cheered.

Upon witnessing her daughter sailing through the air in her undies, Mother Annie nearly fainted right there on the spot. Rastus caught her as she sank down weakly on the grassy bank, her hand covering her mouth. She was shocked beyond words to see her young daughter doing such a dangerous, unladylike trick. "What's the matter with you, Laura?" she yelled when she had somewhat recovered and saw Laura's black head bob back up to the lake's surface. Proper young ladies don't go swimming!" She cried out. "And they surely don't display themselves in their underpants! You're going to break your neck doing such stunts!" She scolded. "What is going to become of you? And where is your sunbonnet, young lady?"

Laura was finally able to squeeze in a response, as she laughed and treaded water. "But it's so much fun, Mama! If the boys can do it, why can't I? And I can't wear my sunbonnet in the water!"

"It's all right, Miz' Tilton," Old Rastus tried to comfort her exasperated mother. "Don't worry; I'z watching little Laura so she ain't gonna git hurt and I gots her sunbonnet right here."

Mother Annie finally retreated to the house, shaking her head and wondering whatever was going to become of her strong-willed, tanned, tom-boy daughter. She was sure that no proper gentleman would ever choose her daring girl for a wife and she would be doomed to life as an 'old maid'. When Mama later told Pa, he just laughed and slapped his knee with pride! Then, he commented that if Laura had been born a boy, rather than a girl, she would surely have become a sailor and gone to sea.

"No, Pa, I would be a privateer just like you and Jean Lafitte!" Laura would answer staunchly and grin.

Yes, Laura was a true daughter of Charles Tilton, the sea-loving buccaneer. I was proud to belong to her and loved her all the more because of her courage and her wonderful, independent personality in the days when it was not encouraged in women.

*****

During the trip, Ben also told about the first time he knew that Laura would grow up to be a free-thinking, self-sustaining woman.

During the summers, after school was dismissed, Mother Annie would always let eleven year-old Laura sail back to Galveston with Ben so she could help Henrietta with their four little girls. Like today, Laura was a tall, slim girl who laughed often and spoke her mind easily, her green eyes sparkling with confidence and the girls loved and respected her. Henrietta enjoyed having Laura come and stay, so paid her well to take care of their daughters.

Laura had always loved sailing and could steer the schooner as well as a man! She was always eager to go because she adored her little nieces and she loved the sea like Ben did, although she was seventeen years younger.

Ben and Henrietta often laughed while watching her, running along sunny Galveston Beach, shockingly suntanned and

Laura Running Along Galveston Beach

barefoot, with her ankle-length skirts tied up and her long, unbraided hair loose and blowing about in the wind. The prim, proper ladies, strolling on the beach in their bonnets, often gasped wide-eyed at the scandalous sight of a free-spirited girl flying by with exposed ankles and loose hair waving in the Gulf breeze!

*****

I knew that Laura, now grown, was very happy and loved her life as a wife and mother, but her misty eyes, as she listened to her older brother, told me that she treasured those times long ago. She looked out at the wide, slow-moving river that had always been a part of her life, and smiled to herself.

Galveston Bay was as smooth as glass when the schooner reached the mouth of the mossy, tree-lined Trinity River and sailed into it under a cloudless, blue sky. Laura opened the picnic basket and took out fried chicken, biscuits, apples from her own tree and, of course, her delicious teacakes.

"Brave Aunt Laura, will you take the helm so I can eat some of that delicious smelling chicken?" Daniel begged. He licked his lips as he inhaled the scent.

"Aye, aye, Captain," she answered and laughed. The girls giggled when their mother gave her nephew a sailor's salute.

No one minded that it took over two hours to cross the beautiful bay. Dan showed them how to trim the canvas sails and how to tie square knots that would never come undone. Tomboy Daisy, who was holding me, tossed me high into the air toward Effie.

"Here, Effie, catch your doll!" Before her sister could complain, Daisy had climbed halfway up the mast of the schooner to check for a sliver of land on the distance. For several minutes, she slowly scanned the horizon from east to west and back.

"Land Ho!" Daisy suddenly shouted and quickly shinnied down to the deck. Soon, the boat pulled up to the Galveston pier.

"You kids walk on to the house with your mama while we unload the rice and your baggage. We'll be home in about ten shakes of a sheep's tail," Dan said, grinning. He dropped the anchor and threw the rope over a piling while Ben rolled in the sails.

Ben's wife, Henrietta, her daughter, Rachel, and the grandchildren, Glen and Janie, had been watching for the boat from the big, attic look-out window that overlooked the bay. Glen had seen Ben's schooner as soon as it docked and ran on ahead. The women picked up their long skirts and hurried down the street behind him, waving as they went. Henrietta loved children and was excited to have their laughing and chattering in her big, yellow, clapboard house.

Ben and Henrietta's Big Yellow Home

"Henrietta, it's so good to be back at my summer home again," said Laura, referring to the summers she had spent growing up here. She handed Donnie over to her sister-in-law's waiting arms and turned to greet Henrietta and Ben's daughter and her children. "You look wonderful, Rachel, and little Janie gets prettier every year! Glen, you've grown taller!" Then, she gave them all big hugs.

That night, Effie let Janie hold me while they snuggled down with Daisy in a fluffy, feather bed on the second floor of Ben and Henrietta's three-story house. I listened to them giggling and whispering in the darkness while the soft, cool Gulf breeze drifted in through the second-story, open window. The white lace curtains fluttered like gentle butterflies, hovering over the happy little girls.

It was so good to be back in my beloved first American home again! How I wished I could turn back time, so this would still be my home and Laura my little owner.

Panther Prowling the Gulf

CHAPTER 3:

A Giant Panther Prowls the Gulf

7:00A.M.~~Galveston, Day Before the Hurricane

The house was still quiet, so Henrietta Tilton relaxed and sipped one more cup of coffee before she started her daily chores. Then, she got up from the kitchen table to clear away the dishes from husband Ben, and son Daniel's, early breakfast. She poured heated water from the kettle on the wood stove into the sink, grated some of her home-made lye soap into it, and swirled the warm water with her hand. Watching tiny, luminous bubbles foam over water, she basked in contentment, thinking how good life was for them here in beautiful Galveston, Texas, and how good it was to have family visiting.

They lived near the populated eastern end of the island, not far from the beach and the Gulf of Mexico on the south side and only four blocks from the bay on the north side. Galveston was fast growing into a large, important seaport and many people were flocking here to live and work. There were many new businesses, a thriving bank and even an opera house called The Grand, all interwoven between tall, waving palm trees.

The Tilton's three-story home served as a look-out on the island, rising above most of the other homes. Henrietta had first chosen white paint for their house, but then decided to go with the cheery, light, yellow paint. She wasn't sure why, except that it would make it easy for Ben's customers to identify their home and it just seemed right. Ben had been pleased with her choice. If it pleased Henrietta, he was happy with it. Ben and Father Charles had built their big house, along with hired help. It served as a home and, from the third floor, as a lookout post over the bay and the gulf for incoming and outgoing ships. Charles, and in later years, Ben ran the hauling and loading business from his nearby pier on the calm, bay side of the island.

Growing up, the children had often climbed up to the third-floor attic to watch ships from different countries entering and leaving the seaport. They had learned to identify the ships' home ports by their flags as the boats sailed through the channel and into Galveston Bay from the gulf. They also liked to watch the beacon at the top of the Bolivar Point Light House as it swept back and forth over the water. The rhythmical beam of light from the black, iron tower guided ships through the channel and into the bay.

Henrietta's parents had wanted a better marriage to a wealthy suitor for her, but had finally given in to their daughter and Ben's deep love. She knew she could never have cared for anyone else as she cared for her sweet, sea-faring Ben, the son of Charles Tilton, a one-time buccaneer who sailed with Jean Lafitte.

She and Ben loved the town and the people here, who were as warm and friendly as the island's climate. The years of raising their older son, Daniel, and their four little daughters, Rachel, Julia, Margaret and Nora, and of having Ben's little sister, Laura, stay during the summers and help with the young girls, had flown by. It was the perfect arrangement for Henrietta, Grandmother Annie, now a widow, and young Laura, who loved staying on the island with her cousins and enjoyed earning some money for her school clothes.

Daniel was now grown and engaged, though still living at home, and all four girls and Laura, were also grown up, with children of their own. They gathered together often for visits at Ben and Henrietta's, and the couple was thrilled to have them back home again.

The barking of a nearby dog jolted Henrietta back to the present. She glanced out of her kitchen window that faced south toward the Gulf. She tucked a stray strand of graying hair behind her ear and a wrinkle crossed her forehead as she stared at the sky. There were dark clouds lining the far-off horizon and a wind was beginning to blow from that direction. By the time Henrietta finished the dishes, a light sprinkle had begun to fall and the clouds had drifted a bit closer. "Curious weather for the end of summer," she thought as she dried her hands. "Rain usually moves in from the east this time of year—not from the south."

Henrietta's daughter, Rachel, and Laura came down the stairs laughing and walked into the kitchen. They sounded much like they did when they were teenagers! "It looks like the children will have to play inside this morning," Henrietta picked up the coffee pot and poured a cup for each girl. "Let's get the board games out of the attic." she added.

A little later, the three women headed up to the third floor attic to look for some games, but when Henrietta passed the round, lookout window that faced south toward the gulf, she stopped short. "Laura, Rachel, come and look at the sky! It's darker out on the horizon than it was a little while ago and the Gulf waves are kicking up." She hurried across the room to the large, bay window that faced north towards Galveston Bay and the mainland.

Rachel pointed. "Look, Mr. Cline, the weatherman, just lowered the white, fair-weather flag at the dock and he's raising the red flag." Staring through the bay window, the women could just make out the tall, dignified weatherman, who was bending over the flag ropes.

Henrietta was concerned to see that the tide was rising. "And there are people still out there surf fishing and watching the waves!" She frowned, thinking about the strong riptides caused by rough waves that rolled in then slid unnoticed back out to sea under the new, incoming waves. The big waves could easily knock a person down and the rip-tide could drag him out to sea in just a few moments. Children raised on the coast were taught to be aware of strong currents and rip tides and to stay out of big waves.

Having grown up on the coast, Laura and Rachel knew well that the red flag meant *storm or gale warning*. "And there aren't any seagulls flying," Laura commented as she looked at the sky. They also knew that birds, unlike many people, always found shelter before bad weather.

"Well, it can't be too bad or Ben and Dan wouldn't have sailed the schooner across the bay and up the rivers to The Cove for the season's last haul," practical Henrietta reassured them. "I believe we are just in for a heavy rain this morning. It will probably pass over and the sun will come out by this afternoon." She wasn't worried because Ben made his living from the sea and was very cautious, especially since their son, Daniel, had joined him in running the hauling business. He had become almost as good a sailor as Ben.

The three women didn't notice Laura's youngest daughter, eight year-old Effie, standing in her long, white nightgown in the attic doorway, dangling me by one arm and listening to their conversation. Seeing her mother's worried face, little Effie quietly tiptoed back down the stairs.

8:00A.M.~~Galveston, Day Before the Hurricane

Henrietta left Rachel and Laura in the attic to look for the board games while she came down and slipped out onto the front porch. She picked the rolled-up morning newspaper and the two quarts of milk left earlier by the milkman.

Through the parlor window, Effie and I could see her neighbor, cheery, stout Flossy MacClenny, who was also out in her yard feeding Silky and Fluffy, her two chickens.

Henrietta waves to her neighbor, Flossy MacClenny

"Sure 'nuf luuks like we're in for a large blow and some rain this day," she called in her heavy Scottish brogue.

Effie whispered to me in her soft voice, "She's from Scotland across the ocean, Annabelle." I wasn't sure where Scotland was, but from her accent, thought it must be quite far away.

Henrietta stopped for a minute to visit her sweet immigrant neighbor, in America only a year. She knew Flossy and her family were not used to the gulf storms, so reminded her to shut and lock her shutters. "If you and your family get worried, come over to our house," Henrietta urged. "We've weathered many a storm in this old house."

Flossy shook her head and thanked her neighbor and they waved to each other again. Henrietta could not know that this would be the last time she would see her neighbor, Flossy MacClenny, this side of Heaven.

Henrietta came back into the house just as Effie slid silently onto the bench behind the kitchen table. She brought in the bottles of milk and the newspaper and set them down on the table. Both Ben and she always watched the weather because he and Daniel spent so much time sailing the schooner back and forth across the vast Galveston Bay.

Something just did not seem quite right this morning as she spread the city paper out on the table. She was thumbing back and forth quickly through the pages and then her eyes fell on a short article. There, on page three, was a small column reporting that a hurricane had moved over the Caribbean island of Cuba, and was now "prowling the Gulf of Mexico like a giant panther," as the editor described the storm. It was expected to turn eastward toward Florida and then move on out into the Atlantic Ocean. Henrietta read it aloud softly, then folded the paper and quickly tucked it into the dishtowel drawer.

"No need to upset anyone unnecessarily with hurricane talk. This is just a summer storm," she murmured to herself and rubbed her chin with her finger. Then startled, she noticed Effie holding me and tried her best to cast a little smile toward my young mistress. Effie smiled back, not quite certain what a hurricane was, but glad that this was only a summer storm.

* * * * *

9:00A.M.~~Galveston, Day Before the Hurricane

The distant rumble of thunder awoke Laura and Rachel's other children. Daisy, little Donnie and their cousins, eleven year-old Janie and her eight year-old brother, Glen, came straggling sleepily out of their bedrooms just as Laura and Rachel placed the games on the kitchen counter. The children were used to coastal storms, so were not at all afraid, only curious. Daisy helped little Don downstairs to Laura. "Come on, punkin', let's go eat breakfast." Daisy talked a steady stream to her little brother.

"Bekfast, mama, bekfast," he chanted over and over until Laura sat his bowl of oatmeal and spoon in front of him. Donnie clapped his hands and began gobbling it up.

"Well, there goes our bicycle ride to the beach this morning!" Glen complained and scowled. Since automobiles had not been invented and horses were expensive to keep, everyone who lived on Galveston Island rode bicycles or walked.

Rachel gave her son a stern look, but Henrietta knew well how to smooth ruffled feelings. "Don't you worry, Glen, we will find something fun to do here in the house this morning and we'll go riding this afternoon." Her words seemed to calm Glen and everyone else, as they usually did.

Hurricane Lamp

The sky was now cloudy and the tide was splashing higher onto the beach. Henrietta lit several hurricane lamps to brighten the house and everyone's mood. These lamps were known as 'hurricane lamps' because they were always used during bad weather as well as nightly. They were made up of a round container, which held kerosene or oil, and a flat rope that was threaded through a spicket fastened on top of the container. The lamp would continue to burn for a long time because the bottom of the wick was soaking in the oil. A tall glass globe was fastened to the top of the container to make the light brighter. Thus, a hurricane lamp would light an entire room.

"Come to breakfast! I have biscuits, eggs, sausage and three kinds of my homemade jelly," Henrietta called pleasantly.

"That sounds great. I'm starving!" Chubby, blue-eyed Glen, always eager for food, suddenly forgot his disappointment about the bicycle ride and rushed to the table.

"Janie and Daisy, will you set the table and, Glen, will you pour the milk, please?"

"Yes, Ma'am," the three older children answered politely. The girls got up from the table and went to the cupboard to get out the dishes, glasses and silverware while Glen got a pitcher of cool milk out of Henrietta's new icebox, which held two big blocks of ice in the bottom to keep food in the top section cold.

Little Effie continued to sit quietly on the bench behind the table, rocking back and forth and holding me. Then, she announced knowingly, "It will be all right. It's just a summer storm and the sun will be out by this afternoon. Then, we can all go to the beach and pick up shells," and she continued to rock me as if to comfort herself and me as well.

Something, though, in my porcelain bones made me shiver. I began to wish we had all gone to the safety of The Cove with Ben and Daniel earlier today. Or better yet, that we had not sailed to Galveston yesterday for this last summer vacation at all.

"Annabelle," whispered Effie. "Would you like to go to the beach, too?"

It was considered perfectly natural in 1900 for young girls to talk to their dolls as they played with them but Glen, being a boy, rolled his eyes and made a face. Effie grinned sheepishly, but continued to include me in her conversations because she was used to her brothers teasing her about her dolls.

Little Effie called me by my American name, *Annabelle,* which her mother, Laura, had given to me long ago when she first received me from Henrietta and Ben for her eleventh birthday. As they did every summer, Ben and Henrietta had invited Laura to come and stay with them and help take care of their four daughters. Laura loved the girls and could hardly wait for school to be out every May so she could go to Galveston Island.

During that summer of 1871, Ben and Henrietta gave Laura a birthday party and a very expensive gift that she would treasure—me. Before that summer and before Laura, however, I had quite another name and lived in a far, faraway country called Germany, beyond the great Atlantic Ocean.

CHAPTER 4:

Annabelle: Long Ago and Far Away

February 1871~~Frankfurt, Germany

I was originally named Anjabel, 'Fraulein (Miss) Anjabel Brigetta,' to be exact. Frau Anjabel Schneider and her husband, Herr Jonas Schneider, lived in a faraway country known as Germany in 1871, and it was she who created me. Frau Anjabel was known far and wide for her porcelain doll-making skills and her good husband, Herr Jonas, was just as famous for his handmade wooden toys—elegant rocking horses, carriages with doors that really opened and shut, and three-story doll-houses. Together, they owned a very successful store called 'Schneider's Doll & Toy Shop' in the center of the big, bustling city of Frankfurt.

The plump, jolly, gray-haired lady had an odd little habit of talking constantly while she worked—to her husband, to the dolls, or just to herself. It didn't seem to matter at all to her who was listening. All of the other dolls often made fun amongst themselves of her steady clatter, but I found that if I listened carefully to her, I could learn a great deal because, in spite of her curious ways, she was a very smart woman. One day while painting our faces, she began to tell us dolls the story of how we had been created:

> *"One cold, wintry day in February, 1871, the old couple received a large order for dolls from Madame Claudette's Dress Shop in Paris, France. Madame Claudette, a quite famous dressmaker, needed twenty-four porcelain dolls of excellent*

quality to fill an expensive order from a doll shop in a place called Galveston, Texas in the faraway new country of America. They were asked to make the dolls as quickly as possible and send them to her shop in Paris. There, Madame Claudette and her staff of sewing girls would make fancy outfits for each of the expensive dolls and then send them on a ship to America.

"That very evening, after the last customer left, the excited, old couple closed their shop and went straight to the back room and set about to work. Frau Anjabel mixed water and fine porcelain clay powder together in a big bowl, while Herr Jonas laid out the plaster-of-paris molds into which the mixture would be poured. The molds had been specially made for doll heads and shoulders, arms, and legs with tiny shoes. Frau Anjabel carefully poured the clay mixture into the molds, one at a time, while Herr Jonas shook them gently to remove bubbles. Slowly, they moved along beside the long worktable, replacing the clay and water mixture whenever it ran out. Then, the clay mixture was allowed to thicken in the molds and, at just the right time, the excess was poured off, leaving a thin layer behind that was stuck to the molds. This layer of clay would become the hollow body parts.

"This pouring process had to be done with great care and took several days to complete. The next evening, Frau Anjabel and Herr Jonas carefully turned the molds upside down on the worktable so that our damp, gray body parts gently loosened and fell out onto it to dry.

"While Frau Anjabel worked on the clay parts, cutting away the seam lines that had been left from the molds, Herr Jonas cut out the dolls' bodies from sturdy, white muslin cloth."

The next day went by slowly because I was so excited for evening to come so that I could hear the rest of the story. Finally, the sun set and the shop closed. Frau Anjabel entered the room, put on her apron and sat down at the worktable. She frowned as though trying to remember the story, then smiled and picked up right where she had left off the evening before:

"All the pourings were finally completed and our clay heads, arms and legs sanded ever so lightly to remove the seam lines. Afterwards, we were placed in the kiln, a big oven that stood in the middle of the workroom. We were carefully arranged on the kiln shelves so that our parts would not touch each other and stick together. Herr Jonas brought in wood for the kiln and arranged it in the bottom. They began to talk about ways to put the money they would earn to good use, if we did not crack during the firing.

"Frau Anjabel instructed Jonas to make the fire big enough so that it would burn throughout the night and turn our clay into porcelain. He lit the wood shavings he had sprinkled beneath the logs and closed the kiln door. The damp clay pieces slowly began to dry and harden as the heat rose. The happy couple hugged each other in the satisfaction of a job well done and went to the kitchen to celebrate with a pot of hot tea.

"The next morning, they opened the kiln door and the sunlight came streaming in. A very strange thing happened when those early morning rays fell upon us. At that precise moment, we began to awake for the first time. I would say, looking back, that February morning in 1871 was my first day as a porcelain doll—my birthday!"

All twenty-four of us lay there without a single crack, although we still needed to be painted and assembled. No longer gray clay, we had turned into hard, snow-white porcelain. Sights and sounds were still hazy to us, much the same as for newborn babies, I suppose, but I could hear the voices of the old couple as they laughed in delight. They carried us carefully to the work table, both declaring that we were the most perfect dolls they had ever made! Then, Jonas went to gather sawdust to stuff our bodies while Frau Anjabel opened their shop.

I was about to drift off to sleep again when I heard a strange, but very pleasant, sound. I learned later that the sound was Frau Anjabel humming a little tune. She hummed often throughout the day, stopping only when customers entered the shop. I came to love hearing

Frau Anjabel's happy voice and then, a moment later, hearing her extend a friendly greeting to the customers. Something about these simple sounds made me feel warm and happy. I had no way of knowing that many times later in my life, wonderful memories of those familiar songs and my Germany home would comfort me greatly and give me needed courage during difficult situations.

Later that afternoon, I awoke and heard the old couple talking about something called *snow*. The air had grown colder, the sky had clouded over, and something white was falling to the ground. From the worktable where I was lying, I could vaguely see the big flakes through the window as they floated slowly down. They began to fall faster and thicker, covering everything in a beautiful white blanket.

Business finally slowed to a halt as people hurried to their homes, so the shop was closed early. The Schneiders hurried into the work room and put on their aprons. Frau Anjabel hummed a little tune as she got out the porcelain paint and brushes. Admiring us once more, she sat down to begin painting us with porcelain enamel. I never knew whether she realized that we could understand her plainly, but she did talk to us as though we were the children she had never had.

Every evening for a week, she carefully painted our arms, legs, hair, faces, and shoes. As each doll received her blond hair, blue eyes, and pink lips and cheeks, she became capable of seeing and speaking (to the other dolls) quite well. Of course, all dolls are created knowing the unwritten rule of never speaking to humans, although among ourselves we are able to converse quite freely.

At last Frau Anjabel picked up the final doll, ME! "Look, Jonas, this doll is the most perfect—my very finest one!" She began to skillfully brush paint onto my face. I felt extremely proud until she said something that struck horror in me! "I believe I am going to paint this beautiful doll differently. I am going to give her black hair and sea-green eyes."

"What are you saying?" Herr Jonas blurted out in disbelief. "Little German girls and dolls here have blond or light brown hair and blue eyes. Who would ever buy such a strange doll?"

I cringed at the terrible thought of no one wanting me. *No, no, please, don't paint me differently! Please!*

Porcelain Doll Head

"Well, since these dolls were ordered from America, perhaps there will be a little girl there who has black hair and sea green eyes," she retorted. "I think the doll will be beautiful! My dear Grandmother Brigetta, who came all the way from Russia to work as a palace servant, had black hair, green eyes and light skin and she was beautiful."

Although Herr Jonas shook his head and frowned, I became the only one of the twenty-four porcelain dolls who was different. Frau Anjabel smiled to herself as she painted my hair, eyebrows, and eyelashes coal black and my eyes bright sea-green. Next, she carefully brushed pink rouge paint for cheeks and lips and painted my tiny shoes black to match my hair. Whispers and rude giggles that Frau Anjabel was unable to hear passed from doll to doll. I wanted to call out to her that this was a terrible mistake—that I didn't want to be different or strange but she could hear nothing that came from my mouth.

"We shall see, we shall see!" bragged Frau Anjabel. She clicked her tongue and smiled proudly. She carried us to the kiln and placed us onto the top shelf for a quick, last firing, which would keep the paint from ever coming off. Jonas brought wood and built a fire in the bottom of the kiln once more. The door closed and warm darkness surrounded us as we drifted off to sleep again.

The next day, the shop was closed, so the old man and his wife could work on us all day and into the night. They removed us from the kiln again and filled our muslin bodies with sawdust. "My wonderful dolls," Frau Anjabel exclaimed. "Now all that each of you needs is a gorgeous dress from Madame Claudette's famous dress shop!" She kissed each one of us and then picked up her smallest paintbrush again. In what seemed to be an afterthought, she said to me, "Because you are my favorite, I am going to give you my grandmother's name. You shall be *Anjabel Brigetta*."

She wrote the name on my muslin back, then turned me over and painted a tiny red heart on the left side of my muslin chest. Finally, she kissed me and handed me to her husband, who gently rolled a sturdy, canvas packing cloth around me, just as he had with the others, and placed us side-by-side into a wooden crate filled with sawdust. We were finally ready for our long boat ride down the river to Madame Claudette's in Paris, France.

"Auf Wiedersehen, dollies," Frau Anjabel whispered softly. She wiped a tear from her eye with the corner of her apron and sighed. "May you have long and happy lives."

"Good Bye, Frau Anjabel, I will miss you," I called, hoping she could hear me. I felt sad to leave our makers, but hoped that her wish for us would come true.

As Herr Jonas nailed the top onto the crate he said, "Goodbye, darlings. May each of you have a special little girl to love you for many, many years." Then he lifted our crate up into his wagon. I could hear the sound of the horse's hooves on the cobblestone street as he drove us to the river dock. There, we were loaded onto a riverboat which, that same day in March 1871, set sail down the great Rhine River to the country of France. We felt a little sad leaving our doll makers, but were also excited about going to the famous Madame Claudette's for beautiful clothes and then, on a huge wooden ship to America. And that was how my very adventurous and amazing life began.

* * * * *

12:00 Noon~~Galveston, Day Before the Hurricane

Laura and Henrietta went back up to the third-floor attic to have another look out of the bay window. They were amazed by what they saw. When they came downstairs, Laura quietly pulled Rachel aside, out of earshot of the children, and told her that the wind was increasing and waves had now completely covered the beach. They exchanged concerned looks, although they knew that Father Charles had built this home well and it had withstood many storms over many years.

Ben and Henrietta's house, in the middle of the seaport town, was near the east end of the island at the harbor entrance, like the rest of the town. And, like the other houses, their big, yellow house stood four feet above the ground, elevated in case of flooding. Only the Tilton house, however, stood on the original, cement foundation that had been built by the pirate, Jean Lafitte, for his Galveston headquarters. Despite this knowledge, I still felt uneasy, because this could be a very bad storm.

"I think it is better to be safe than sorry. We don't want that wind to blow any glass into the house. Let's shut and lock all of the window shutters while Rachel keeps the children entertained," Henrietta whispered to Laura.

While Laura and Henrietta closed and latched the wooden shutters, Rachel sat down at the big kitchen table and opened the Chinese Checkers and Tiddly Winks games. "Who wants to try to beat me?" She challenged Effie and Daisy, laughing. The excited children scrambled up to the table to play.

The wind continued banging against the shutters and it wasn't long until Henrietta slipped back up to the attic to peek out of the lookout window again. I knew she was wishing that she could see Ben's boat, *Black Jack II*. When she came back, she suggested that they take the children and games up to her large, second-floor bedroom. Laura sensed her anxiety, but cheerfully led the children upstairs. She urged, "We'll play dress-up and have a party!"

"Do you hear that, Annabelle?" little Effie asked me. "We might even dress you up."

I cringed because a very bad memory from long ago of being dressed up flashed through my mind.

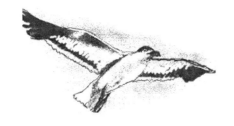

CHAPTER 5:

Annabelle's Memories: What Shall We Wear?

Dear Reader:

Has anyone ever hurt your feelings very badly? Dolls know how that feels, too, but we are not able to cry. I wish we could because it seems that crying makes humans feel better. But, since I cannot shed tears, I must just sit there feeling ashamed, hurt and alone.

Truly yours, Annabelle

* * * * *

March, 1871~~Paris, France

What should have been a nice boat trip from Frankfurt, Germany, to Madame Claudette's Dress Shop in Paris, France, was quite a torturous ride for me. Although I didn't realize it, the other dolls in the crate were extremely jealous that Frau Anjabel had called me the most perfect doll and had given me her name. As they whispered amongst themselves, I commented excitedly, *"I can feel the boat rocking in the water."*

Instantly, at least half a dozen dolls snapped back at me. *"Be quiet, ugly servant doll! You're different!"* Then they all laughed. I cannot actually remember any more of their conversation or even the rest of the boat trip because I was so hurt by their cruel words. I do remember that I did not say anything else for the rest of the trip to Paris.

We finally reached Paris, France, and our crate was carried to Madame Claudette's. Several young ladies spoke French as they eagerly pried off the top. "Ooh la, la!" one of the young seamstresses exclaimed when she began unwrapping the dolls.

"The dollies are magnifique!" Several of the girls squealed and clapped their hands.

Madame Claudette was extremely pleased with our beauty and quality. "Oui, Mais Oui! Yes, oh, yes!" she repeated, unrolling doll after doll. At last, she picked me up. I hoped she would say something nice about me, but instead she remarked, "Look, girls! Whoever heard of a German doll with black hair and green eyes? Everyone wants German dolls who are blonde-haired and blue-eyed!" She turned her thin lips down and shook her head fiercely.

The young ladies quickly agreed and all tittered among themselves. To my embarrassment, I felt the critical eyes of the other dolls upon me and was sure I heard them snickering, as well. Then, mercifully, Madame laid me back down in the crate where I could remain in darkness and out of sight a little longer.

I finally realized the truth and it hurt terribly—I was ugly! If she had thrown me on the floor and shattered me into a hundred little pieces, I could not have felt worse. Frau Anjabel had made a terrible mistake by painting my hair black and my eyes green! I knew at that moment that no little girl would ever want me and that I would always be alone and unloved. For a doll, that is the worst possible fate, ever.

All the following week, we lay on Madame's long worktable awaiting our turns for her to choose crisp, shiny taffeta or soft, rich velvet for just the right dress. Her helpers made white, muslin camisoles with ribbons and lace on the front and pantaloons with tiny lace edging around the ankles for us. Then they dressed us in stiff, white cotton petticoats with full skirts to make our dresses stand out, which was the fashion of the day.

When each doll's outfit was completed, she was placed on Madame Claudette's special sewing table. She studied every doll carefully and then, chose the perfect dress material and colors for her. Under Madame's skilled hands and expert eyes, the girls cut out beautiful doll gowns from expensive silk, satin, and velvet materials. Afterwards, they sewed the splendid red, pink, royal blue, forest green, and lavender outfits with her newest mechanical, foot-treadle sewing machines.

As each doll was finished, Madame examined it and handed it back, telling the girl what accessories to add. Some dolls received pearls or rhinestone necklaces and earrings, while others got little hats with pretty feathers, and still others, parasols, satin ribbons or lace. One by one, each doll began to look as though she were ready to step onto a palace ballroom floor, as Madame Claudette's sewing shop was transformed into a brilliant kaleidoscope of colors that seemed to sway and glisten under the oil lamps.

High Fashion Doll In Madame's Shop

Finally, she picked me up from the bottom of the crate. I had hoped that she would just forget me, but no, she began to search for suitable cloth for my dress. Shaking her head, she looked at the youngest seamstress sitting near her. "Perhaps a more simple fabric, Madame," murmured the girl shyly.

Madame nodded, got up and went to the back room. In a few moments, she returned with a yard of pale blue cotton material covered with little pink flowers. "I hear there are pioneers in America who wear cotton gingham and sunbonnets." Madame said, "Perhaps one of their daughters would like a doll dressed like that." She raised her eyebrows and sniffed haughtily. All of the shop girls giggled at the thought of a common pioneer girl.

My dress and a white muslin bonnet were quickly cut out, sewn and fitted on me. I didn't get feathers or lace or even jewelry, but at the last minute Madame Claudette hurriedly tied a blue ribbon around my waist. "There, little country doll, you are now ready for a hardy American pioneer girl!" She held me up high for the shop girls to see. Of course, everyone, including the other dolls, laughed at my plain cotton dress and muslin, pioneer sunbonnet.

Just then, a tall boy entered the shop to get the crate ready for shipping. He carried a box of tools in his arms. "Bon Jour, Pierre," Madame greeted him and the young ladies all giggled again, repeating her good morning greeting. He blushed and stammered as Madame continued, "I am just now getting ready to pack the dolls back into the crate." She dug down into the sawdust in what seemed to me an attempt to hide me at the bottom. So hasty was she in wrapping the packing cloth around me, that she didn't even cover my head! She packed all the other dolls and scattered sawdust over us to keep us from breaking during the long Atlantic Ocean journey.

Pierre painted words on the crate's top, reading them aloud as he printed. At last, he nailed the top firmly onto our wooden box and lifted it up into the back of his horse cart.

CONTENTS: PORCELAIN DOLLS
DESTINATION:
MISS JOSIE'S DOLL SHOP—-GALVESTON, TEXAS AMERICA

"Take the crate to the Seine River Dock and pay the barge captain for transporting it down the river to the seaport." I could hear Madame Claudette counting out coins to him. "Don't forget to bring the change back to me," she added.

"Oui, Madame," Pierre answered, as he climbed up into the driver's seat of the cart and signaled the horse to go.

As he pulled away, Madame called out to us, "Bon Voyage, Mademoiselles. Have a good voyage!" The young shop girls, following her cue, giggled again as they called out goodbyes to us and to Pierre, who was no doubt blushing.

All the other dolls were sad to leave Madame Claudette's Dress Shop. They had enjoyed the royal attention they had been given. I must admit that I was glad to get away from the bossy, arrogant woman, but I didn't offer my opinion. We were now about to begin the second leg of our journey—the boat trip to America.

* * * * *

2:00PM~~Galveston, Day Before the Hurricane

Laura helped little Donnie get dressed. I was lying on the bed beside him. The cousins were all talking at once, wanting to know why they were dressing up. Henrietta replied hastily that they were going to have 'dress-up party and a fancy picnic in her big, second-floor bedroom.' "Ben and Dan will be home soon this afternoon to play too," she added trying to sound cheerful. "Now everyone hurry and finish getting dressed."

"Can Annabelle come too?" asked Effie. She held me up to Henrietta. Smiling at her little niece, Henrietta tousled her hair and nodded.

Glen started to say something, but changed his mind when the girls gave him dirty looks. He realized that he was outnumbered by girls and better just go along with them and dress up for their "tea party."

While the children were dressing, I could hear Henrietta quietly telling Rachel and Laura that the waves were beginning to lap up on Beach Street, the street that ran along beside the Galveston beach. "Now, I don't want you to worry because this house has withstood many storms, but Ben always likes us to be cautious." Henrietta comforted the women.

She decided to send Laura and Rachel back down to the first floor to gather up anything they could find that might be useful for the day and night. Rachel returned with a basket filled with the leftover breakfast sausage, several loaves of homemade bread, a jar of jelly, some apples, and the tin of Laura's teacakes while Laura came back with two jugs of water, a hurricane lamp and a can of lamp oil. She had also noticed the oilcloth on the kitchen table and had grabbed it along with some matches. Henrietta went down to the back porch and brought back rain slickers, jackets, some coiled rope and an extra quilt. Lifting their long skirts, they each hurried, in turn, up the stairs with their loads. Then, they spread out the oilcloth and the picnic on the spacious bedroom floor.

Henrietta could see that Daisy, Glen and Janie were starting to wonder why they needed to stay on the second floor of the house. She pulled Laura and Rachel aside and asked them if they could think of anything that would distract the children for the time being. Suddenly, Laura remembered the old trunk in the attic. It held mementos and clothing from years gone by. "Why don't we open that big, green trunk and they can try on the old clothes and shoes?" she suggested.

Henrietta and Rachel's faces lit up. "What a wonderful idea!" answered Rachel. She lit the hurricane lamp to take up to the attic with them. The children, with Cousin Janie now carrying me, and the women all headed up the stairs to find the old trunk.

The big trunk had been Henrietta's wedding gift when she and Ben had gotten married, given to her by her parents. She hadn't opened it for years and was surprised to see the many forgotten dresses, handbags, hats, jewelry and shoes that spilled out. "Oh, here are the button-up shoes and the veil I wore for my wedding." She held up the white high-top shoes. Grinning, Daisy reached for them. Everyone laughed because Daisy usually showed more interest in guns than ladies' clothes.

"Janie, Daisy, Glen, look at me!" shouted Effie. She modeled a large-brimmed hat, a purse and long gloves. "I'm a very fine lady." She strutted around the room, her small, turned-up nose stuck up into the air and everyone laughed.

Janie had found an old fox fur stole and put it on with a long skirt and some jewelry. "Oh, this is so much fun, Aunt Henrietta. Thank you for letting us try on these things!"

Glen pulled out a hat and clomped around in Ben's old boots. "I'm Papa," he sniffed haughtily and tried to look stern.

Janie Tries on the Fur

"Me Papa! Me Papa!" Little Donnie repeated over and over when Glen set Ben's old cowboy hat on his head. It tipped down over Donnie's right eye and ears but he didn't mind one little bit!

"Mission accomplished," Laura whispered. The women chuckled and nodded in satisfaction, knowing this activity would keep the children busy for at least an hour or so.

4:00 P.M.~~Galveston, Day Before the Hurricane

Later that afternoon, a buggy pulled up in the heavy rain to the Tilton home. It had crossed the newest marvel, a wagon bridge that spanned the water between Galveston and the mainland on the Houston side. The man got out, tied the horses to the hitching post and bounded up to the door. Rachel heard his calls and ran downstairs to throw open the door. "Harvey, you're supposed to be at home," she said, surprised to see him here. Her husband came in and gave her a big hug, although he looked troubled.

"I could see the bad weather moving in from our house and was worried. I thought I should come to get you and the children a day early; that is, if you don't mind."

Rachel answered him and patted his arm. "Well, this seems to be just a heavy thunderstorm, but I know you're concerned. If you think it best, we will cut our vacation short and go back with you today. Harvey had not been raised near the coast and always tended to worry about bad coastal weather and possible hurricanes. Laura and Henrietta had come downstairs and heard the conversation. They crossed the room and warmly welcomed Rachel's husband. Without arguing, Henrietta headed back upstairs with Rachel to pack the children's things.

Harvey urged Laura. "You are all welcome to come home with us. And there's plenty of room in the buggy. If this turns into a hurricane, you will be safer on the mainland. The water has already covered Beach Street and is coming into the yards."

Rachel's Husband Drives Buggy to Galveston

"Thank you, Harvey, but Ben and Daniel should be here any minute and will expect us to be here waiting. If they think there is any danger, they will take all of us back across the bay to The Cove. There have been no hurricane warnings, so this is surely just a summer storm and, besides, this old house has gone through many a storm with high water." She smiled, then wondered why she felt slightly nervous.

Henrietta came down with the last of the bags and hugged her daughter and grandchildren. "Chin up," she grinned. "We will all get together again at Thanksgiving. Won't we?" Laura and Rachel nodded vigorously and hugged each other.

Harvey nodded and smiled, but glanced cautiously out toward the bay. He would feel safer when his family was off this island and he wanted to cross the bridge before water covered it. He quickly picked up the satchels and ran with them out to the covered buggy. The children unhappily told their cousins and grandmother good-bye and soon they were all waving from the buggy as the horse headed toward the only bridge between Galveston Island and the mainland.

8:00 P.M.~~Night before the Hurricane

Henrietta had decided to have a slumber party to cheer the children up in her big, second-floor bedroom that night. They piled quilts and pillows on the floor and played charades and board games and told stories. Henrietta produced a sack of lemon drops that, along with the tin of Laura's teacakes, made perfect snacks. This party, so familiar to coastal children, was called "riding out the storm" and was meant to be exciting and fun, so they wouldn't be afraid. Little Don had a great time too, shouting and jumping, but finally wore himself out and dropped off to sleep. I sat on the big oak dresser and enjoyed the party, but I could hear the wind blowing stronger and stronger and could see the periodic worry cross the faces of the women because Ben and Daniel were not yet back. All was not as festive as it seemed to the children.

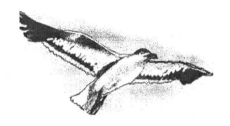

CHAPTER 6:

Annabelle's Memories: Perilous Ocean Journey

We were about to embark on a wonderful adventure. It was almost too much to believe! I was thrilled and hopeful, so I tried to forget that the other dolls didn't like me. Has someone ever made you feel bad about yourself? Dolls cannot cry but we know how it feels to be sad and hurt. I remember Frau Anjabel saying that life goes on and time heals all hurts. I shall see if this saying is true. If the saying is true for me, then it should be true for you as well.

Your friend, Annabelle

* * * * *

April, 1881~~From France to America

At the Seine River Dock, I could hear the boy as he paid the barge captain. "This crate of dolls has been ordered by a doll shop in America. Madame Claudette needs a receipt from you." Then I heard Pierre thank the captain and turn his horse and cart around for his trip back to Paris.

Soon the barge began its journey with our crate and many others down the long Seine River to Le Havre, a busy seaport on the Atlantic coast of France. Our crate was by no means watertight, having slits between some of the sideboards. I had been jostled about during the cart ride just enough to be able to see out through a half-inch crack between the two bottom boards in my little corner. It made an excellent window through which I could see the tall Poplar Trees that lined the river bank. As people bundled coats and shawls around themselves and hurried along the path, their breath came out into the cold air in round white puffs because of an early spring freeze. The barge continued down the great river, slowly passing other boats along the way.

Men Loading The Medallion for the Atlantic Journey

When we reached the port of Le Havre, the crates bound for America were lifted off the barge and stacked on the wharf where we waited to be put aboard a ship. At dawn the next morning, I could hardly believe my eyes when I peeked out through the small opening! We were beside a large harbor filled with boats and ships going to and fro. The water was dark blue with patches of sunlight shimmering on the tiny ripples.

There beside the wharf a wooden ship, larger than anything I could have ever imagined, was docking. The name painted on the side of it was *The Medallion*. Men shouted orders back and forth as they rolled up white canvas sails and tied them to three tall poles called masts. An order was called to lower the anchor and the ship stopped moving. Another order to lower the gangplank resulted in a walkway being let down from the side of the ship to the wharf.

Along with hundreds of other boxes, our crate was hoisted up with ropes onto the deck of *The Medallion*. It wasn't long before I could hear the sailors yelling out the numbers and names of crate contents as they lowered the boxes into the ship's hold. There were tools and hand-carved furniture, smoked salmon, cloth, French hats, dresses, button-up leather shoes, books and many other things that I cannot remember. Our doll crate was finally wedged in tightly between all the other goods bound for America.

Thankfully, the other dolls, busy with their endless gossip and haughty criticism, seemed to have forgotten about me, so I lay quietly in the bottom of our crate. Since they usually thought only of themselves, perhaps they would not remember "Anjabel, the ugly servant doll in plain pioneer clothes," during the long trip across the ocean.

Early on a cold morning a few days later, the captain shouted, "Hoist the sails, mates!" "Heave Ho the anchor! Steer to the starboard! Let's get underway while this 'ere tide is still high enough to take us out!" I could hear scuffling as the sailors jumped into action and I suddenly felt the great, wooden vessel slowly slipping out of the harbor as a cheer went up among the crew.

"Aye, Captain, she be catching a good breeze, she is, and all 'er sails are filling out!" came a shout.

On the twelfth day of April 1871, *The Medallion* moved out into the vast Atlantic Ocean for her two-month crossing to America. Never in my wildest dreams did I think I would ever have such an adventure! It was so exciting that I forgot all about my looks. I could hear the huge canvas sails flapping loudly in the early morning breeze and smell the fresh scent of the salty sea spray.

Although the other dolls whispered and made fun of the uneducated sailors, I thought they sounded very smart about ships and oceans. In fact, I learned a great deal of information and many stories by listening to them. We were following the southern trade winds that blow from east to west carrying our ship to the new country. On the ship's journey back to France, they would follow the route of the northern trade winds, which blow from west to east. Someone said that the great explorer, Christopher Columbus, himself, knew about these trade winds and used them to make his seven trips to the New World and back to Europe.

The trip across the ocean took many long days, during which the sailors worked very hard. But on nights when the work was finished and the weather was good, we could hear them up on the deck singing, playing harmonicas, and strumming guitars. These tough men seemed to enjoy their seafaring life and joked and told stories about their exciting adventures. I was often lulled into a peaceful sleep by the strains of *Oh, Susannah*, *Jimmy Crack Corn* and *Yankee Doodle Dandy*.

Three times *The Medallion* ran into storms, *squalls* as the sailors called them, but I will never forget the most terrible storm of all. The sailors worried among themselves when they saw the sky beginning to blacken. The wind began to blow very hard and ear-piercing thunder roared overhead. We rocked back and forth from stern to bow and from side-to-side until the ship groaned and shuttered as though it were being torn apart. I thought we were surely going to sink beneath the giant waves that splashed against the ship's sides.

The captain shouted orders to lower the sails and lash them down so they wouldn't tear apart. Heavy rain pelted the ship and poured through cracks in the deck floor into the hold splashing over many of the boxes below. The thunder roared and fierce lightening crackled and hissed as it hit the nearby water and lit up our dark quarters. Screams rose from our crate with every frightening bolt, although no one could hear our cries. After a long while, the storm spent itself and the sea grew calm again. The sailors raised the sails again, a fresh wind filled them out, and we were on our way once more. I slept most of the way since I was at the bottom of the dark, cramped crate.

Some days I could hear dolls complaining. "Ohhh, my velvet dress is being ruined by this wretched dampness!"

"Well, I am well-wrapped and my dress is fine. I will certainly be purchased by a wealthy princess!"

"No, I'm the most beautiful doll here," said another. "I am sure a royal queen will take me home to her palace for her daughter!"

Frau Anjabel and Herr Jonas Schneider had often spoken of the new land across the Atlantic, so I could have told these haughty dolls that there were no princesses or queens, kings or even palaces in America. However, they would not have believed me and, mercifully, seemed to have completely forgotten about me so I said nothing. I was left alone, hoping against hope that some little girl would want me for her very own.

The month of May passed slowly and then, one day early in June, I heard a sailor high up in the crow's nest call out, "Land Ho to the West!" Then we heard men from every part of the ship running to the bow. A great cheer went up among them as they spotted a thin sliver of land on the horizon!

"America, my new home," I thought. For the hundredth time, I wondered if someone here would want an ugly black-haired, green-eyed doll in a pioneer dress and sunbonnet.

Our ship finally reached the coastline of America, then turned southward toward a place the sailors called the "land of the flowers" or Florida. The weather became warmer as *The Medallion* rounded the tip of Florida and sailed into the warm Gulf of Mexico. All the while, the other dolls grumbled that the heat was definitely damaging their expensive dresses and argued over who had the most beautiful outfit. I would be glad to be away from their whining and bragging. We stopped briefly at the large seaport of New Orleans, Louisiana, where most of the loaders spoke French, to my surprise! Canned goods, ladies' fashionable dresses and shoes from France, and some building tools were unloaded there. Then we sailed on to our final destination, the busiest port on America's gulf coast, Galveston, Texas.

* * * * *

Friday~~The Cove, Day Before the Hurricane

Ben and Daniel later told everyone about their hauling trip. Like most other days, they had left early to make their scheduled boat trip across Galveston Bay and up the Trinity River to The Cove community.

They had seen some darkness on the Gulf horizon as they sailed the schooner from the dock out into the bay, but the sun was shining and a good breeze was blowing. Since only the Galveston weather station's white fair-weather flag was flying when they pulled away from the dock at seven o'clock, they contentedly ate the biscuits Henrietta had sent with them. A south wind (that was blowing in ahead of the storm) filled out their sails and pushed them across the bay and into the mouth of the Trinity River at top speed. Sure enough, at ten o'clock that morning, they pulled up to The Cove dock.

After docking the boat, they walked up the riverbank to Mother Annie's house. She was surprised to see them so early, but directed them to sit down and have a glass of tea while she fried fish and potatoes for her son and grandson. She still lovingly called them 'her boys' even though they were quite grown. Ben and Dan were bragging on her meal, so she proudly told them how she had taken her cane pole and gone fishing early that morning and had caught some perch just in time to clean them for their dinner. By afternoon, the sky began to cloud up over The Cove and Ben told her about the worrisome, distant clouds out in the Gulf this morning.

Mother Annie said, "I reckon we are in for some rain. All the area farmers are finishing sacking up the last of their rice for you to take back to Galveston tomorrow and sell." She urged them to get up early the next morning and 'shove off to get home in case a squall was setting in.' Ben nodded, knowing his mother was wise because she had helped his father make his living from the sea, too. Ben and Dan spent the rest of the day loading the big tow sacks into the schooner as each farmer drove to the river dock with them.

CHAPTER 7:

SUNSET RED, SAILOR'S DREAD

6:30A.M.~~Galveston, Early Morning of the Hurricane

Ben awoke Saturday morning to the sound of wind blowing and a light rain falling on the tin roof of his mother's big farmhouse at five o'clock. He awoke Daniel and they quickly got dressed. Mother Annie was already up and preparing their breakfast. She tucked a bottle of hot coffee and some cornbread wrapped in a napkin into Daniel's hands and the men hurried down her sloping backyard to the loaded schooner.

The journey was very slow on their return trip due to the storm's south wind blowing against the schooner. As they sailed out of Old River, into the Trinity River and then out into Galveston Bay, a very unusual event happened—the wind suddenly changed and began blowing from the north towards the bay and the Gulf! As the sails filled out and increased their speed, they began to see the big, angry, black clouds covering the sky above Galveston. Ben had rarely seen such a wind change to that direction before a storm on the bay. He was solemnly aware of how serious this situation could be, even though there had been no storm news from the weather station during the last week.

Ben remembered seeing a red sunset when he was loading on the Galveston dock two days ago. He now repeated to Daniel the old saying Father Charles had taught him years before. *"Clear sky, sailor's delight—Sunset red, sailor's dread."* He suddenly and painfully realized that, although he had noted the flag on the wharf weather pole indicated fair weather yesterday morning, for the first time in years, he had not glanced at the barometer in the parlor before leaving home. The weather had been so nice when he and Dan left for the dock that he had simply forgotten. Now, he felt foolish and irresponsible because he knew better than to ignore nature's warnings.

* * * * *

9:00A.M.~~Galveston, Morning of the Hurricane

Daisy was the first to wake up to the sound of the shutters banging against the house the next morning. Then, she heard the shouts of young people outside. She jumped up and ran up to the attic to peer through the bay window shutters. She could not believe her eyes when she saw people frolicking in the streets and yards that were filled with water. They dodged waves and ran this way and that. When the strong wind would knock them down, they would get right back up and start playing again. Even some of the ladies were out with their umbrellas wading, laughing and kicking water at each other. It wasn't long before the rest of the family had followed her up to the window. Henrietta shook her head, knowing that these foolish people were taking their lives in their hands.

"Mom, can we go out and play in the waves? Please! See, everyone is outside having fun. Please!" Daisy begged. Laura told her that she could not go out because it was dangerous, but she continued to plead as only a headstrong child can and Glen and Janie followed with pleas of their own. Henrietta looked at her sister-in-law and decided it was time for them to hear the truth.

"I have something to say to all of you, she said firmly. Sit down." Surprised by her tone, Daisy, Effie, Glen, Janie and even little Donnie dropped immediately to the floor. "We have been treating you like little children. Now, we are going to treat you like the young ladies and gentleman that you really are." The children straightened their backs and leaned forward.

Laura, Effie and Glen Watch the Storm

"Those people are very foolish to be out in this bad storm. They are ignoring the power of the sea. This is no longer a rainstorm or a gale, but a *hurricane*! I did not tell you last night because I didn't believe it, but the barometer does not lie. Look at the one here on the wall. See, the needle is always pointing to 30 when we are having good weather. When it falls to 29, clouds move in and we have rain or a storm. It has now fallen to 28.90, which puts it into the hurricane zone. We must use our wits, stay inside this strong house where it is safe and we must not take any risks. Most importantly, you girls must obey us without question or complaint. Our very lives may depend on it!"

When she finished her speech, the children's eyes were wide with alarm. "A hurricane!" They repeated, wide-eyed. Suddenly, Daisy jumped up and ran to Laura, hugged her and cried, "I am sorry for begging, Mother. I will do whatever you and Aunt Henrietta say, and I won't complain again." Henrietta hugged Laura's precious children, too, knowing she had touched the right chord in strong-willed Daisy to bring forth the responsible young woman inside this adventurous girl. She knew that she had frightened them, but decided it had been the right thing to do. Satisfied, she looked at Laura, who nodded in complete agreement.

"But, Mama, what about Uncle Ben and Dan?" asked Effie, clutching me tightly.

"Now don't worry your head about Ben and Daniel," answered Laura. They will be here as soon as they can. If anyone can sail in rough water, it is Ben!" Then, they all turned away from the window and went back down to Henrietta's big bedroom to play games.

* * * * *

12:00 Noon~~Dangerous Journey Home on Day of Hurricane

Ben sent Daniel below to check the boat's barometer, hoping that it might give them an indication of how bad the weather was becoming. *Black Jack II* had been through many a storm over the years with Ben's father and then with him at the wheel, so he wasn't too concerned; however, he knew that Henrietta and the girls would be worried about them. When Daniel came back up on deck, Ben donned an air of confidence. Daniel anxiously reported to his father that the barometer on the boat's wall had fallen from the stormy weather reading to a hurricane reading of 28.85. He brought back two slickers from the hold. He handed one to his father and put the other on himself.

"Don't you worry, Dan," he said in a light-hearted, but tense, voice and tousled Daniel's hair. "With this hard wind pushing us, we'll be home before you know it. Hold the rudder steady and keep us straight on course!" Ben was thankful for this tailwind because it should help them cross the stormy bay in just a few hours.

He yelled to Daniel to hoist the remaining smaller sail, hoping they could pick up even more speed. Standing fast at the helm, he later sent his son back down into the hold a second time to check the barometer. Bounding back up to the deck Daniel cried, "Pa, the barometer is still falling. It's down to 28.80! Should we turn back to The Cove?"

Dan had not been out in the boat during many bad squalls and Ben could see the worry in his son's eyes as he took hold of the rudder handle.

"This seasoned old schooner has handled a lot worse than this!" He forced a laugh.

Ben now knew that this was more than a storm, but he decided against using that dreaded word *hurricane* just yet. Going back to The Cove was not an option with the women alone at home, so he continued the course toward Galveston. Besides, Father Charles' old barometer could be giving a false reading, although he knew better today.

The waves steadily rolled higher and higher, until they were splashing onto the deck of the *Black Jack II*. The schooner would rise high up on a big wave with its bow pointing toward the heavens, then, as the wave passed beneath it, it would teeter on the top like a toy boat on top of a mountain peak. Then, the wooden schooner would groan and plunge downward into the trough, as though it were going to dive to the bottom of the sea. The swells kept increasing in size and anger by the minute, until Ben began to fear for their lives. Every wave threatened to be the final yawn that would swallow the schooner.

Having been a pirate who sailed the seas, Ben's father Charles had taught him the best sailing tactics. One suddenly popped into his mind. To keep from sailing head-on into the huge swells, the boat's course could be set to steer diagonally to the left, then changing to the right, and then back again. Using this zigzag pattern of sailing should keep the pounding waves from breaking the schooner apart and prevent it from taking on too much water and sinking. Over the roaring wind, he cried out to his son that they were going to make it. Using this spark of knowledge, Ben became more hopeful and set his mind and face toward home.

* * * * *

2:00PM~~ Galveston Island, Afternoon of the Hurricane

Mr. Cline drove his horse-drawn cart through the heavy rain and flood water back and forth along the beach street where many people from the town had gathered to watch and play. He yelled over the wind for them to leave and get to higher shelter, but most of them paid no attention. The wind continued to increase with every hour. Only a few people had left the island before the bridge and the two railroads that stretched to the Houston mainland had fallen into the bay this morning.

We later learned that the Galveston Weather Bureau Official, Mr. Isaac Cline, received a hurricane warning by telegraph from the National Weather Bureau in Washington D.C. It stated that the hurricane had turned west and was somewhere in the Gulf near the Texas coast. Mr. Cline was able to send out one emergency telegraph message to Houston's weather station. Just as he finished clicking the Morse Code message, the wind snapped the telegraph lines—Galveston's only link to the mainland. Of course, no rescue ship could sail to the island anyway, through such bad weather.

3:00PM~~Galveston, Afternoon of the Hurricane

At three o'clock that afternoon, Isaac Cline, with no thought for his own safety, rode his horse through the swirling two-foot water to the dock for the last time. The wind and rain had now grown to such intensity that there was no doubt. This was a bad hurricane. From the attic bay window, Henrietta saw the slumped figure as he sadly raised the red flag which had a black rectangle in the center—the dreaded hurricane flag. It was, however, already too late for anyone, even his own family, to leave Galveston Island. Henrietta felt sorry for Mr. Cline because he was a good, responsible weatherman. People would probably blame him for not knowing about the storm earlier, but no one was at fault.

"What was it Ben had said? 'Hurricanes are like great silent panthers stalking the seas, quickly turning this way and that, but always going wherever they wished,'" thought Henrietta. If only Mr. Cline had known earlier this morning and had raised the storm flag sooner, Ben would have noticed it. She knew that he would have insisted that all of them, even their neighbors, sail across the bay to the safety of The Cove. But there was no need in crying over 'spilt milk!' She hoped that he and Dan would stay at Mother Annie's and not return to Galveston, but she knew in her heart that Ben and Dan would not leave their family here alone in such a bad storm. The waves were now swirling and tossing their whitecaps high into the air. As the water became more violent, it made sailing dangerous, but if anyone could make it across that bay, it would be Ben, son of a seagoing pirate.

Henrietta quietly comforted Laura. "Our house is well-built of strong cypress wood and has weathered many storms because it sits on the strong, thick concrete foundation that was Jean Lafitte's. We have seen storms that have caused brick buildings to fall and, yet, our house still stands. We will be all right."

Laura agreed that she was right. And Ben would surely know that they would lock the shutters, go upstairs and "ride out" the storm in their big, strong, yellow house. The people of Galveston, although not yet afraid, were beginning to realize that this was no ordinary storm. Many in houses less well built took their families and trudged through the knee-deep water to one of the several brick buildings downtown or to a friend's stronger house. Others simply did as Henrietta did: ushered their families upstairs, and hoped the treacherous storm with its pounding rain and lightning would quickly pass over.

CHAPTER 8:

Annabelle's Memories~~
Dry Land at Last

I had been surprised to learn from listening to the sailors that there are many different kinds of people in America. They have different colors of hair, eyes, and skin because they came from many different countries. It seems that it is all right to be different in this big new country! People here are respected for their good character more than for their riches or fine clothes and there are no kings or queens. A great leader of my new country, President Abraham Lincoln, has freed all of the slaves and declared that everyone in America is equal. America is a free country and I think I will like it here. My hopes rise as I dream of a little girl who will want a doll who is different. I did not know that my wish would very soon be answered.

Very Kindly Yours, Annabelle

* * * * *

June, 1871~~Dolls Arrive in America at Galveston, Texas

According to the sailors, the twenty-seven mile-long, three mile-wide island of Galveston was once deserted except for some Indian tribes and a den of pirates led by the famous Jean Lafitte. It was now becoming a busy seaport with ships moving in and out loading and unloading goods. There was even a railroad and a bridge now running across the bay to a muddy, Texas town named Houston and a ferry running to Bolivar Point. When our ship finally reached Galveston Bay, the sails were rolled up and the anchor was lowered into the water to hold the ship fast so it wouldn't drift. There, *The Medallion* sat in the harbor and awaited its turn to have the wares from France unloaded.

The next day, the sailors suddenly began yelling, scurrying about and hoisting crates up from the hold. Our crate was moved up on the deck and I could see bright sunlight through the little crack in the box. I could tell that a lot of work was going on. Men drove horse-pulled wagons out into the water up to the horses' chests because Galveston did not yet have a long pier. The sailors unloaded crates from the ships into small boats and rowed them to the wagons. As their wagons were filled, a bearded man, who seemed to be in charge, shouted commands to the horses and other drivers as they made their way back to the sandy shore. The wagons were unloaded on the beach, and then driven out into the water and filled with crates again. This activity went on all day under the clear summer sky until there were many piles of crates on the sandy beach.

Unloading ships in Galveston Harbor

Our doll crate was one of the last to be lowered into a rowboat and then lifted onto a waiting wagon. After the horses had pulled the wagon back to shore, we were placed on the beach. I was very happy to be on solid, dry land and for the long ocean journey to finally be over, and I was excited to watch the men working through the slit in my box.

After two months on the vast Atlantic Ocean, it felt very good to be in this new land, even if the seaport here was just a sandy beach on the island of Galveston, Texas. Through the little crack in our crate, I could see and hear the man in charge shouting again to his workers to check off the crate numbers as they were unloaded. The dark-haired man had a short beard and tanned skin from the sun. He yelled over the wind, "This stack of crates goes to Houston. That furniture goes to Morgan's Store on Fourth Street. Take the boxes of cloth and shoes to O'Gill's Mercantile Shop! Henry and James, all the food products go to Roushea's General Store on Seventh Street!" The workers nodded in understanding and began to load crates into the wagons.

Most of the crates were already gone by the time they noticed our small one. "Mr. Tilton, what about this crate of dolls?" a big, strong, black man, wet with sea spray, grinned and pointed toward our wooden box.

"James, I'm glad you spotted that little crate. Those dolls are bound for Miss Josie's Dress and Doll Shop," replied thirty year-old Benjamin Tilton, the owner of the hauling service. He paused a moment then called a boy named Daniel to his side.

I later learned the background of this Tilton Family, who was to become my very own family, so I will share it with you now.

Father Charles Tilton was a Pirate

Ben and Laura's father was Charles Tilton, one of the first settlers in the Trinity River area here on the Texas coast. After being captured by rogue pirates and taken to Galveston Island, Charles was taken in by Jean Lafitte and the boy accepted an offer of a job sailing with him. He liked the seafaring life of the buccaneers and planned to save and purchase his way back home to New England later. But, Charles fell in love with the privateering, swashbuckling life and stayed with Lafitte for six years of adventure!

After the pirates disbanded, Charles returned to New Hampshire to visit his family, but came back to Texas because he loved the land. He had obtained a grant from the Mexican government for one thousand and five hundred free acres near the coast. Charles married and used most of the gold doubloons he had earned to build a house for Annie Barber, his new wife, and to buy a schooner and start a hauling business. They raised nine children including their oldest, Ben, and their youngest, Ben's little sister, Laura, on the lush farm and ranch land along Old River, a tributary of Trinity River.

Ben Tilton, Charles' Son

Ben grew up, was now married to Henrietta and had four little girls. He loved Henrietta's son, Daniel, as his very own son and the boy loved him as his father. Dan, as everyone called him, also loved the sea and helped in their loading business. When Father Charles had retired, Ben took over their hauling business and hoped that one day he could pass it on to Dan.

The Trinity River flowed out into Galveston Bay and the farmers who lived along the coastal river needed someone to transport goods to market for them. Ben and Daniel brought sacks of rice, bales of cotton, vegetables and even cattle to Galveston to be shipped on to other markets for them. They also hauled tools, food, seeds, and other things to the farmers from the port of Galveston. Sometimes they even carried passengers on the boat. It took almost a day to cross Galveston Bay, so they often stayed the night at the Tilton homestead with Mother Annie and Ben's brothers and sisters.

Mother Annie Tilton

Annie Tilton still ran the farm and the busy boat dock in back of her house with the help of Ben's younger brothers and sisters and several freed slaves, who had stayed on after the Civil War as hired hands.

Ben and Daniel always looked forward to hauling day up the Trinity and Old Rivers so they could spend time with the family.

Mother Annie was known as the best cook in The Cove area and always had the big oak table spread with a bountiful supper. After the food had been blessed, they sat down to a home-cooked feast of smoked ham or sausage from the smoke house, fried chicken or catfish, vegetables picked from her garden, and hand-ground cornbread with fresh-churned butter from their cow, Betsy. Jars of wild plum jelly, blackberry jam and homemade pickles always sat in the center of the big oak table.

Just when everyone would think they couldn't eat another bite, Mother Annie would bring in a big chocolate cake or pecan pies and steaming cups of coffee. It was a regular weekly feast and reunion, where the family talked and joked and Ben caught up on the latest happenings in The Cove. Most of the people who lived in the area were kinfolks and those who weren't, were good friends. Hauling day was the happiest day of the week for Mother Annie because she loved having her children and grandchildren visit.

June, 1871~~Daniel Opens the Doll Crate on the Beach

Through the small crack, I could see a tall, lanky boy as he walked across the sand to Ben, startling him out of his daydream. Ben instructed, "Dan, go ahead and open this doll crate. We need a birthday present for Laura because she will be twelve years old tomorrow. See if you can find a pretty doll she might like."

The handsome boy grinned widely, showing perfect white teeth, and quickly found a crowbar. He began to pry the top loose from the crate. Every doll held her breath! Which one would he choose? "No doubt he will choose me because I am the prettiest," bragged the pompous doll dressed in forest-green velvet.

The blue taffeta doll responded arrogantly, "Are you blind? Can't you see that I have a gorgeous beaded dress and my hat is made in the finest Parisian style?"

Within a few minutes, all the dolls were arguing with each other. The doll, who seemed to be the leader, screamed at them. "You stupid dolls! My dress and parasol are made of red silk, spun from threads of rare silk worm cocoons, found all the way around the world in the country of China. Madame Claudette even told me that I am unusually beautiful. So there! That settles it!"

The dolls continued to murmur among themselves until the boy brushed aside the sawdust and unwrapped the first doll. He looked at her blonde hair and blue taffeta gown. She sighed angrily as he put her down. Next he picked up the green velvet doll, and then laid her aside. I heard her say, "Humph, Commoner! This stupid boy doesn't even recognize true beauty when he sees it." Next, he began unwrapping another one.

Haughty Doll

Everyone held their breath when he inspected the red silk doll, for they were sure he would choose her. But he set her aside, too. "Ignorant boy, you must know nothing about quality and finery. I shall just wait for the royal Princess of America to choose me!"

"Pa, these dolls all have blond hair and blue eyes," he said. "No, this one won't do either—too fancy for Laura." Daniel knew Laura well. He unwrapped more of the dolls, carefully studying each one, before he wrapped her back up again and laid her aside.

Finally, he reached the bottom of the crate where I lay. I shuttered! I did not want him to see my ugly hair, green eyes, and plain cotton dress. But, as he picked me up and unwrapped me, his eyes opened wide, and I could tell that he liked me.

He yelled, "Father, come and see this one! Laura's going to love her. Look, she even has a dress like Laura's and a sunbonnet and black hair and green eyes like her!"

Ben Tilton walked over and looked at me. He nodded and grinned. "She's perfect, Dan. Great job! Now, pack up the other dolls and take the crate to Miss Josie. Ask her to charge this black-haired doll to my account." The other dolls lay beside the crate in disbelief and seething anger, pretending not to notice that I had been chosen. I didn't mind though, because I was so happy that my sawdust stuffing was about to burst!

By late evening, *The Medallion* had been completely unloaded and Ben and Daniel Tilton walked home together. As the bright orange sun began to sink into the Gulf, the western sky turned a brilliant red with lavender clouds, and I could hear the seagulls flying low overhead. Ben remarked that they had done a good day's work and patted Dan's shoulder. "Pa, the sunset is red! You've said that a red sky in the evening means stormy weather."

Ben studied the sky carefully. "Yes, usually," he said as he stroked his short beard. "Father Charles taught me this years ago. It pays to keep an eye on the sunsets but, at this time of year, it probably just means rain tomorrow, but between August and November, we must be very cautious because of hurricanes."

"But Pa," asked Daniel, "Aren't there other signs that a hurricane is coming?"

"Hurricanes are like big, strong panthers sneaking over the water. They are hard to predict, but the seagulls know when one is coming and they fly to the mainland just before one hits. Most people don't pay attention to this sign, though, and I fear that many people would not leave since a bad one has not hit the island, that I can remember."

I listened intently to this interesting conversation between the two men. Their talk continued about these storms that seemed to be common in the Gulf of Mexico, as Ben spoke about how they started like a rainstorm far out in the ocean. Then, they turned into great storms that stretched for miles, and started swirling around and moving faster and faster until they finally hit land and caused a lot of rain and flooding.

Daniel nodded in agreement then asked, "What if a hurricane hits now?"

"Well, there have been improvements—a long dock and pier, and a bridge and railroad line now stretch from the island across the bay and all the way to Houston. And don't forget Isaac Cline, our good weatherman and the telegraph warning lines!"

Still noticing the worried look on Daniel's face, Ben added, "Now don't you worry! We keep an eye on the barometer at our house just in case the needle should start dropping. If one were headed this way, we would leave Galveston and sail up here to Mother Annie's homestead where it's safe. Hurricanes spin themselves out after they hit land, so they don't bother towns inland much, except for bad rain."

"You just get that doll out of sight," instructed Ben, changing the subject. "Laura's birthday is not until tomorrow, and we want this doll to be a total surprise for her!"

My heart skipped a beat! Who would have ever thought that I would be a gift? It was all I could do to keep from shouting and laughing; I was so happy! Even Frau Anjabel or Madame Claudette could not have imagined my good fortune.

* * * * *

4:00P.M.~~Galveston, Afternoon of the Hurricane

After their dangerous crossing of Galveston Bay, Ben and Daniel sailed *Black Jack II* into Galveston harbor. Daniel lowered the riggings while Ben dropped the anchor into the water and tied the boat to a piling. They both climbed out onto the pier and trudged through the heavy, stinging rain with their heads down. They knew from past experience where the buildings stood along Bay Street. Holding their arms out in front of them, they managed to get to the first structure. Finally feeling the wall, they inched their way through the semi-darkness and now waist-deep water. The streets were deserted except for several other pitiful passersby making their way along the buildings like Ben and Dan. The wind was now blowing at gale force, flinging stinging salt spray into their faces as they stumbled slowly on through the flood.

Suddenly, a board came hurling through the air and hit Ben's head with such force that it knocked him to his knees. Dazed, he struggled to get back up, but couldn't raise his head above the water until Daniel helped pull him to his feet. "Dan, you go on. I can't make it!" yelled Ben. Determined not to let go of his dazed and bleeding father, Daniel shook his head stubbornly. Slowly, they continued wading along the pitch-dark street.

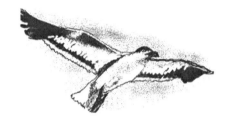

CHAPTER 9:

Annabelle's Memories
"The Birthday Gift"

Someone once said, "Beauty is in the eye of the beholder!" I do believe it is true. What do you think?

Your friend, Annabelle

* * * * *

June, 1871~~Galveston, Texas

Daniel shut the gate of the neat picket fence. As he and Ben walked up the wide front porch steps, Daniel quickly tucked me under his shirt. They stepped inside and Ben opened the big hall closet. Henrietta stepped into the hall and he whispered, "Come see what we have for Laura for her twelfth birthday. This gift came all the way from Germany!" He took my packing cloth off of me and handed me to a plump, rather short lady with black hair piled softly on top of her head.

She gasped in delight and put her hand to her rosy cheek, "Oh, My! What a beautiful porcelain doll! She's perfect. And look, her dress is almost like Laura's." Then, they quickly put me up onto the highest closet shelf quite out of sight.

I lay on the dark shelf until the next evening, when Henrietta opened the closet door. She picked me up and smiled, showing dimples in a sweet, round face. I was very glad that Madame Claudette had not dressed me in the shiny taffeta or rich velvet. My blue gingham dress with little pink flowers and green leaves was perfect for a girl in this new land. Henrietta carefully carried me to the parlor where a big oak dining table spread with a delicate lace tablecloth stood in the middle of the room. Then, she began arranging china dishes on the table. As she worked, she hummed a little tune that reminded me of one that Frau Anjabel Schneider used to hum while she was working.

Birthday Table

As Henrietta placed a box and a blue ribbon beside me (I later found out that blue was Laura's favorite color), the front door suddenly flew open and four giggling girls spilled into the room, all with bare feet showing from under their long skirts. "Mother, Laura took us shell hunting on the beach," one of them announced holding up her apron half filled with seashells." Henrietta quickly put me in the box and tied the ribbon.

I could hear her admiring her daughter's sandy shells, then calling over the noise, "Girls, put your shoes on and wash up for the surprise party!"

"Oh, thank you, Henrietta," her younger sister-in-law replied, as she and the girls hurried back into the parlor.

"Look, Laura, a birthday present!" shouted her four little nieces.

Laura Carrying Little Nora

"I know what it is," teased Daniel as he and Ben walked into the parlor.

"What?" Laura asked, her eyes big with excitement.

"A sweet potato and a switch!" Dan burst out laughing at his own joke.

"Is not!" replied Laura. She tried hard to sound angry, although she seemed to be enjoying his good-natured humor.

"Is too!" he laughed harder than ever, "That's because you've been so bad this year!"

"Here, open your present and find out for yourself," said Henrietta. I could hear the girl nervously untying the blue ribbon from the box. Then she lifted the lid.

"Please, oh please, like me!" I silently pleaded.

A pretty, sun-tanned girl folded back the tissue paper covering me, carefully lifted me up and stared at me, her mouth open in surprise. She had long, black hair and beautiful, sea green eyes. Suddenly, I noticed the tears welling up and overflowing the long lashes of her big eyes, and I was sure she was unhappy with me. Then, the words came tumbling out of her mouth. "Oh, thank you, thank you, Ben and Henrietta! I have never, ever had a real store-bought doll. She is so beautiful! I have always wished for a porcelain doll. I've seen them in the fancy store windows, but never thought I would have one. Oh, this is the best present I have ever received in my whole, entire life!"

Laura hugged me so tightly I thought my arms might fall off. Ben cast a quick glance at Henrietta and she returned it, smiling. They both knew that Mother Annie did not have extra money for store-bought toys since Father Charles had died. But she was a proud woman who had raised nine children and would not ask for any help. Ben always saw to it that she and his little sisters and brothers had everything they needed, but money never stretched far enough for luxuries.

"You can thank your nephew, Laura. Dan picked her out of a big crate of dolls all the way from Germany. Laura ran over and gave Daniel a big hug, causing him to grin and blush. Then, she cradled me in her arms. I suddenly noticed that Laura had on a blue gingham dress with pink flowers scattered on it.

"Henrietta, Ben and Dan, and girls, thank you! She is so beautiful and I will always treasure her." The slim girl held me high to show me off. If it had been proper for dolls to talk to humans, I would have told her that it was she who was beautiful! She had long, shiny, black hair and her tall frame was brown from the sun, much to everyone's dismay, because tanned skin was not at all proper for young ladies in the 1800s. She wasn't as dainty as Henrietta, but had a carefree spirit and an untamed beauty. Her pink lips were full and her mouth wide, revealing straight, white teeth when she laughed, and she seemed to be talking and laughing most of the time. "Whatever shall I name her?" Laura said aloud as she gazed at me.

"Her name is Anjabel Brigetta," Daniel blurted out. "I saw it written on her back."

He reddened and quickly ducked his head when he realized that he had just revealed too much interest in a doll! No one, however, seemed to notice because all eyes were on me!

Laura's nieces were begging for turns to hold me, so she handed me around carefully to each one, introducing me as she went. "Rachel, meet An—An-ja—bel." Laura stumbled over the German pronunciation. "That is a little hard to say!" She thought a moment, then and then finally settling on an English name. "I know! From now on, you shall be 'Annabelle'." So, in an instant, I was renamed *Annabelle*. "Now, Annabelle, meet Rachel who is eight."

Never having seen a porcelain doll before, the short, curly-haired girl stepped up to touch me in wonder. I noticed she had the same big green eyes as Laura. "Annabelle, my second niece is Julia. She is seven years old." A shy smile emanated from Julia's rosy, round face. "And this is five year-old Margaret—well, everyone calls her Maggie and last, this is little Nora who is almost four."

I wanted to laugh as the smallest little girl curtsied, beamed at me and said, "Pleased to meet you, Miss Annabelle." I couldn't help but notice that she slipped a small, sandy seashell into Laura's hand as a gift and that Laura bent down and kissed her cheek.

Ben stood up, grinning. "Look, everyone," he said, pointing toward the kitchen just as Henrietta entered the room with a big, white birthday cake ablaze with twelve candles. "Make a wish, Laura!"

They all cheered and began to sing, "Happy Birthday" to Laura. She shut her eyes, silently made a wish, and blew out all the candles as everyone clapped. Henrietta cut big pieces of the three-layer yellow cake, piled high with rich, white coconut icing, and served them to everyone.

My Introduction to Ben and Henrietta's Daughters

"Thank you all for a wonderful birthday—I will never forget it." Laura held me gently in her arms as she hugged everyone again. I could feel her heart pounding with excitement.

That night when my new owner climbed into bed, she gently laid me on a pillow. "Annabelle, would you like to know what I wished for?" she whispered. "I suppose it is all right to tell you since you can't tell anyone. I wished that everyone could be as happy as I am tonight." She tenderly tucked me in, kissed my cheek, and said, "Goodnight, Annabelle," as she drifted off to sleep.

I had not known what love was before Laura Tilton became my owner, although I had heard the word. Now, I knew that my maker had painted a little red heart on my chest so I could love someone. I was glad now that she made me different from all the other dolls. Over-whelmed with this new emotion, I did something a doll must never do. I whispered softly, "I love you, Laura!" There, I had done it! I had broken the cardinal rule of all dolls, 'Never, never speak to a human.' But I simply could not help it.

I was sure that Laura heard me when her big, sleepy eyes opened wide and she peered at me in the moonlight, then a smile spread across her pretty face. She pulled me close and fell asleep. I wondered if, tomorrow, she would think she had been dreaming.

The soft rhythm of the waves floated gently into the room on the cool, gulf breeze. This was a doll's dream come true—a loving owner and four little girls who all wanted to play with me. I was, at last, the happiest doll in Galveston, in Texas, in America, in the whole wide world! I hoped the other dolls from our crate would find such happiness, too.

* * * * *

5:00P.M.~~Galveston, Evening of the Hurricane

At last through the sheets of heavy rain, Ben and Daniel spotted the small flickering lights of the hurricane lamp that Henrietta had placed in the front window. Exhausted, they stumbled up to the house and pushed open the door. Inside, they were met by everyone with hugs and tears of relief. "Thank the Lord, you are both home safe!" cried Henrietta. She wrapped blankets around the cold, drenched men while Laura ran to the kitchen to make hot coffee. Daisy hurried to get clean towels, iodine and bandages for Ben.

When Ben could finally speak, he said, "Oh, Henrietta, I have done something horrible!" Henrietta's eyes opened wide with fear. "Had he run the schooner aground or hurt someone in the storm? Clearly, he and Dan were both all right."

Without waiting for her question, he confessed, "Mother Annie sent a present with me for your birthday. I'm so sorry, but I reckon I lost it somewhere in the bay."

A wave of relief rolled over Henrietta and she started laughing. Then, everyone else started laughing, too, and they laughed and laughed until tears rolled down their cheeks.

"What on earth is so funny about me losing your present?" asked Ben, perplexed.

"Oh, my dear, sweet husband," she answered when she was finally able to stop laughing. "Don't you know that I don't care about a present now? You and Dan getting home safely are the best birthday presents I could ever receive!" Ben smiled sheepishly and, for a moment, I saw the kind and thoughtful little boy he once had been.

CHAPTER 10:

Ben's Story~~Kidnapped by Pirates

July, 1871~~Galveston

The summer after I had been brought to America and given to twelve year-old Laura was the happiest of my life. She came from The Cove to Galveston every summer to help Henrietta tend to her four little girls. Henrietta repaid her by making her beautiful school clothes, buying her school shoes and giving her a small wage. She and Ben had devised this plan a few years ago because it helped out Mother Annie and Laura as much as it helped Henrietta.

Laura often carried me around as the long, lazy days of summer melted into weeks. In the evenings, after supper, the little girls, Laura, and Daniel would often gather in the parlor on the big rag rug around Henrietta and Ben's rocking chairs for the day's news and for stories. Tonight, Julie was rocking me in her arms, so I was able to hear stories about my new family, too.

Ben took out his pipe, tapped it and filled it. "How would you children like to hear the story about your Grandfather Charles Tilton?"

"Yes, Papa, yes!" they shouted at once. Of course, they all knew the story well but were always eager to hear it again. Henrietta got up, lit the hurricane lamp and set it on the side table. Its burning wick caused shadows to flicker across the wall, which made the mysterious story ever so much better. Ben lit his pipe and leaned back in his rock-

Sailors Going After a Whale

ing chair and Laura snuggled into the corner of the sofa with me in her lap.

1799~~New Hampton, New Hampshire:

"Long ago, in 1799, my and Laura's father and your grandfather, Charles Tilton, was born, the third of ten children, in the Atlantic seaport town of New Hampton, New Hampshire. His father, Green Tilton, had fought in the American Revolution with George Washington to gain freedom from England. Afterward he married and went back to the only job he had ever known—whaling. It was dangerous work, just as his father before him had done, but the love of the sea had always run in the Tilton blood.

"Green signed on with one of the huge, wooden sailing ships that went out twice a year from New Hampton for four-month trips on the Atlantic Ocean. They went in search of the great humpback whales for the precious whale oil that everyone used to burn in their lamps and for making candles. They processed the whales right on the ship, boiling down the fat for oil in a big, covered vat that sat on a metal floor in the middle of the ship. The oil was stored in barrels and the meat was salted down, both to be sold when they got back to port.

"Every year, Charles had begged his father to let him go a'whaling too, but every year, the answer had been the same. 'I need you to stay home and take care of your mother.' Finally one year, after his father had broken his arm in a fall from the roof, fourteen year-old Charles was, at last, given a different answer. 'Son, I reckon you are old enough to find out what sort of work you want to do. I've already inquired, and the Captain of the *Evening Star* is willing to take you on as an apprentice when they sail out.' Charles was thrilled, but his mother was unhappy about her young son going to sea. Finally, however, she agreed.

"Early on the morning of the sailing, he walked down to the dock with his family. 'I'll keep a lamp in the window for you,' Mother said tearfully, referring to the custom of keeping a light burning to guide the whaler home from the sea. Charles kissed her cheek, hugged his sisters and brothers, and for the first time in his life, shook hands with his father.

"'Don't worry, I'll be back soon!' Charles called to his family confidently as he boarded the whaler with the other members of the crew. He stood at the ship's stern waving to them as the huge wooden vessel moved slowly out of the harbor. During that moment, he suddenly felt very small and alone and watched with a tinge of sadness until he could no longer see the white handkerchiefs his mother and sisters were waving. Indeed, that image of his family and their parting words would remain with him always.

"A month later, somewhere off the eastern coast of America, as the crew of the *Evening Star* scouted for whales, a ship appeared on the horizon. High up on the main mast, the sailor on watch in the crow's nest shouted, 'Ship Ahoy!' The captain pulled his telescope out of his coat pocket and noted that it was a sleek schooner flying an American flag.

Using a common trick, the pirates had fooled the captain of the American whaler by flying the same flag. The narrow, long schooner moved much faster than the bulky whaler and, as they came closer, the friendly flag was lowered and the skull and crossbones flag raised.

Although Jean Lafitte, leader of the huge band of men headquartered near New Orleans, Louisiana, had forbidden them to attack American vessels, it was too good of a looting opportunity for the greedy pirate captain, Jay Rooster, and his first mate, Jim Groggins, to pass up!

"There was no way for the whaling vessel to get away from the pirates, so the crew had no choice but to stand and fight. Surrender was not an option because it meant certain death. The captain ordered Charles to get below and hide because of his youth and inexperience, and the rest of the crew was ordered to their battle stations.

Cannon fire was exchanged between the two ships, but the schooner was able to zigzag and avoid most of the hits. When it came alongside the whaler, the pirate captain gave the order to board. Long ropes with hooks were thrown over the whaler's railings, and the gangplank was lowered. Within minutes, the pirates, armed with muskets and swords, boarded the big ship and began fighting in hand-to-hand combat with the sailors.

"It wasn't long before they discovered the boy and took him aboard their schooner. Now a prisoner, young boy stood on the deck of the pirate ship watching the fearful sight. Men shouted as barrels of gunpowder exploded and pistols fired. If it hadn't been for the ball and chain attached to his ankle, Charles would have gladly slipped over the side of the schooner and onto the *Evening Star* to fight with the sailors in their efforts to fiend off the bloodthirsty marauders. Of course, he knew that he would be killed, but what a fight he would put up!

"The mast and sails of the whaler began to burn, a death kneel to any ship. The pirates hurriedly transported crates of food and barrels of whale oil from the *Evening Star* to the *Black Jack*, and then chopped holes in the bottom of the ship. They lowered the ship's lifeboats and

Pirates Attack the Whalers' Ship

made the whalers walk the plank. The sailors and their captain swam to the boats and drifted away. Of course, they had no food or water, so Charles knew their death warrant was surely sealed. As the flaming whaler began to sink beneath the waves, his heart sank with it. Quickly, before there was a chance of being discovered by another ship, the pirates set sail south to their headquarters.

"Charles loathed the schooner's vicious captain, red-haired Jay Rooster, who most likely got his name from his bright reddish-orange beard, huge beak-like nose and a strutting walk resembling that of a rooster. He felt the same intense dislike for Rooster's first mate, Jim Groggins, who had wicked, beady black eyes and a cruel, sneering smile. Charles knew that no one would be able to pay his ransom, so he assumed that soon his own life was about to end. The young boy could never have imagined what the next chapter of his life would bring.

"Rooster and Groggins brought young Tilton back to their headquarters and presented the frightened lad to Jean Lafitte to be used as a ransom. In spite of his fear, Charles could not help but be struck by the appearance of the notorious pirate. He was smartly dressed in a black uniform and a large black hat with a huge white feather attached to the side. His black mustache and small, pointed beard were carefully groomed causing him to look, for the entire world, like an aristocrat. As the two pirates bragged about their attack on the whaler, they failed to notice their admiral's mounting rage. They had disobeyed orders, killed an American crew, and captured an innocent boy! To their total shock, Lafitte ordered that Rooster and Groggins be hung that very day for disobeying his orders, then he warned the rest of the men again to stay away from American vessels.

"The United States Government had an agreement with Jean Lafitte to help keep America's coasts clear of the heavily armed Spanish frigates bound from Mexico back to Spain with their loads of Mexican gold, silver and slaves. For this service, the privateer and his men were allowed to keep any bounty they took from the ships. Lafitte knew, however, that if they returned the boy now, it would be an admission of piracy on an American vessel and the government would turn against all of them.

"The privateer saw that the boy was young and terrified so he had his chains removed and ordered that no harm come to the lad under penalty of death. He took the boy under his wing and offered him a job on his ship as cabin boy. Charles was thankful for his rescue and, being an adventure-seeking teenager, eagerly signed on for the tasks of keeping the admiral's cabin tidy, washing his clothes, and serving his meals. In return, Lafitte paid him good wages, which he saved for his trip home.

"Strange as it may seem, Jean Lafitte was known for his courtesy to ladies and his kindness to children and always treated our father well. Lafitte was well-liked by those who met him.

Only Known Painting of Jean Lafitte
[Courtesy of Lafitte Museum, Huntsville, Texas]

"At first Charles was homesick, but he quickly began to enjoy his new seafaring life, the generous wages and a split of the booty taken from every Spanish galleon. It was a service to the United States Government they were doing, and he reasoned that home and family would still be there when he returned later with money he had earned himself. Charles loved the sea and was treated kindly by all of Lafitte's pirates, so going home became an event in the distant future.

When he had finished his chores for the day, he could roam about the ship, listen to the crew's stories, and learn about the schooner. "There was Stumpy, who had a wooden peg where his left leg used to be. Stumpy taught Charles to read a compass and to steer by the stars. Old Cricks liked to whittle and enjoyed making little animals for "Charlie," as the men called him. Of all the buccaneers, it was Tall Dan who was Pa's favorite. He could dance a jig and do back flips, but what fascinated the boy was his endless tales of adventures, mysteries from faraway lands and stories about Indians. They became fast friends very soon.

"One day, a floating mass of debris was spotted in the water. They sailed closer and realized that it was a boy on the pile of rubble. Charles Louis Cronea, a thirteen year-old French boy, was the only survivor from a storm that had sunk a French merchant ship.

Lafitte also took him in. He joked and said, "This ship will soon become a home for boys if this continues."

"After their work was done, Charlie, as Father was now called, and Louis would talk for hours on end, play rock chess, whittle, and fish. Together, they learned to sword fight and shoot pistols straight. Louis would remain father's life-long friend. Charlie liked all of his new friends and this exciting, carefree life on the sea with the smell of salt spray in his nostrils and the feel of the cool sea breeze blowing on his face.

"Jean Lafitte's band continued to cruise about the Gulf of Mexico, preying on the Spanish Galleons. Because the group declaring allegiance to Lafitte had grown so large, the notorious pirate moved his base to the uninhabited Galveston Island just off the Texas coast in 1816. Charles, now seventeen, was rewarded for his hard work and had risen to the rank of boatswain, an officer in charge of rigging, anchors, and sails and of calling the crew to duty every morning.

"Trade in pirated goods in Campeche, as Lafitte had named their base on Galveston Island, had reached an all-time high. The bay was filled with pirate ships and goods taken on the high seas. Even the warehouses on the island could not hold all the spoils, so boxes and bales were piled high on the beaches. Campeche attracted more pirates and adventurers

Charles & Lewis fighting Hong Kong

and soon became a small city filled with traders, casinos, stowes, hotels and saloons. It wasn't long before there were over a thousand men who claimed allegiance to the now famous French buccaneer and Charles was one of them. Though you won't find it in history books, Lafitte was known to be a kind, generous person, and was a good friend to Pa.

"During the next four years at Galveston, Lafitte's men raided Spanish vessels for the American and Mexican governments, and he built himself a fine home called Maison Rouge, which meant *red house* and set himself up as Governor of the island.

"Pa, now a young man, liked the swashbuckling, adventurous life, stayed with Lafitte for six years and went on many raids with him. By 1820, the Gulf of Mexico had about been cleared of the hated Spanish ships, so the United States Government decided to order the band off the island and away from the coast. Lafitte gave Pa and his other officers, schooners and gold as a reward for their loyalty. Then their infamous friend, Jean Lafitte, sailed away, never to be heard from again.

"Pa, Louis Cronea and several other friends, sailed his boat up the Trinity River and into Old River, which ran through The Cove area. In a small lake, Charles scuttled his ship to avoid detection, then they divided their gold and split it. Later Charles and Louis applied for free land grants from the Mexican Government. Charles chose land around his beloved "Cove" and Louis decided on ranch land near Sabine Pass on the nearby Texas coast. Afterward, Charles traveled home to visit his family.

Charles & Friends at Lost Lake

Our pa returned to his free land six months later and married Annie Barber, who became your grandmother. He built her a house in The Cove on the banks of Old River. Later, he built a second house here in Galveston right on the concrete foundation of Lafitte's Maison Rouge and began our hauling business between the Texas Coast and the Galveston Island Sea Port."

* * * * *

Ben took a puff on his pipe and sat lost in thought. Although he stopped the story here for the night, I later learned the complete story of Charles Tilton, the buccaneer and friend of Jean Lafitte. But that is another story in my first book.

"Don't stop now—tell us some more," everyone pleaded.

"That's enough for tonight," said Henrietta. "Perhaps tomorrow evening, he will finish the story. Now, off to bed with you all!"

"I'll get them to bed and hear their prayers." Laura jumped up and took Nora's hand.

"Whatever would I do without you in the summers?" Henrietta shook her head.

"You would be four times as tired!" called Laura, laughing and looking at little Nora, who was now clutching me.

"Yes, I would," agreed Henrietta. "While you are getting the girls to bed, I'll roll the quilting frame down from the ceiling and make us some tea. We can visit while I stitch on the patchwork quilt."

Laura nodded eagerly. She had helped Henrietta piece the small sections of flowers together for the beautiful "Flower Garden" quilt. Now they were almost ready to attach the backing with cotton batting in between for warmth. Henrietta smiled a secret smile and winked at Ben, who grinned, thinking how thrilled Laura would be when she found out that this quilt was for her very own hope chest! In those days, every girl had a hope chest and filled it with things she and her mother made or bought for the future day of her wedding.

I wish I could tell you that Laura and I lived happily ever after like characters in fairy tales do, but I can't. That is just not the way the human world is. My sweet first owner, Laura, grew up, much to my disappointment.

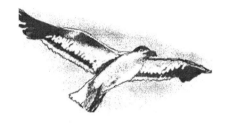

CHAPTER 11:

Annabelle's Memories
"Laura Grows Up"

Did you know that dolls learn things quickly and have extremely long memories with a great deal of patience? Patience is most necessary because we often sit for years on a shelf or lie in a cedar chest when our owners begin to grow up. Eventually, they have little girls or nieces of their own and give us to them. The problem is that we are supposed to love the new owner. But how do we do that when our heart is already filled with love for our first owner?

Very truly yours, Annabelle

* * * * *

June, 1877~~The Wedding in The Cove

Laura still took me with her to spend the summers in Galveston helping Henrietta with the girls, and then brought me back with her to The Cove for the school year. As she grew older, she began carrying me around less and less while the younger girls carried me more and more. Most often, it was Maggie or little Nora who held me. Laura was becoming a beautiful, young woman with more grown-up things to do. Often, after she made her bed, she gently straightened my skirts and sat me on the pillows, or sometimes she placed me high up on the parlor shelf. I particularly liked this vantage point because the family gathered in the parlor every evening and I could hear the news of the day.

I remembered Frau Anjabel talking to me long ago as she painted my hair black. She said that I would, no doubt, have many owners over the years because little girls grow up, but I did not think I could ever love anyone as much as I loved my first owner, Laura.

A handsome, dark-haired young man named Fielden Stubbs, who lived nearby in the small town of Barbers Hill, began courting Laura in 1876. A soft-spoken, polite gentleman, he seemed to care for her a great deal and came often. Although I missed her company, I enjoyed seeing her so happy. Once, I heard Fielden whisper to her that he would love her forever and she answered back that she would always love him, too. Then he did something extremely scandalous during the 1800s. He kissed her cheek!

A year later, Laura and Fielden were married in the little, country church in The Cove. The circuit-riding minister, who rode in on his horse every other weekend to preach, agreed to come and perform the wedding ceremony.

Laura's older brother, Ben, had specially ordered a bolt of pure white silk and had it shipped all the way from New York City. Laura's mother had helped her make a long, white, wedding dress with a high neck and long sleeves. No one in The Cove had ever seen such a beautiful dress. Her sisters picked roses, carnations, and pink hydrangeas from their yards to make Laura's bouquet and to decorate the church. Henrietta helped Laura put her long, black hair up and added sprigs of tiny, white Baby's Breath flowers into it before attaching the white, net veil to her head with hairpins. "There, you look like a sun-tanned angel!" laughed Henrietta, giving her a hug. Indeed, Laura, slim and tall, was extremely beautiful, as Mother Annie often commented, "Pretty is as pretty does," and that fit Laura.

All of the Tilton brothers and sisters and their children, as well as Fielden Stubbs' big family drove their wagons to the church. The building was so full that extra chairs had to be brought in for all the guests. Annie, Laura's oldest sister who was named after her mother, brought sassafras roots she had dug from the tree in her yard, strained and boiled it to create delicious sassafras tea. It made a cool, refreshing drink that they served to the guests to ward off the summer heat.

Laura had chosen her youngest niece, Nora, now ten years old, to be her flower girl and it was Nora who thought to bring me from Laura's bedroom! "Annabelle must see your wedding!" she proclaimed. She pinned a small pink rosebud on my dress and set me in her chair on the front row. Brother Ben, who had always seemed like a father to Laura, walked her down the aisle and gave her hand to Fielden. They repeated their vows before the minister and he pronounced them "man and wife." I had never seen a wedding before and was excited and happy for Laura and Fielden, although I was sad to see that my owner would now be a busy housewife and mother with no time for me.

Afterward, there was a big dinner on the church lawn under the shade of the elm and sweet gum trees. Laura and Fielden sat down with the Tilton and Stubbs families to share their first meal as husband and wife. All of the children played tag and hide-and-seek and pulled sugary sap off the sweet gum tree trunks to chew. Someone got a fiddle out and made the afternoon complete with music and singing. It was a wonderful, joyous day for the new couple and their families.

Fielden and his brothers had worked all year to build a house of sturdy, cypress wood. It sat on a piece of the Tilton homestead acreage that Mother Annie had given them as a wedding gift.

Laura took her big, cedar hope chest filled with dresses, embroidered doilies, tablecloths, the quilt that she and Henrietta had made together and many other things for their new home. She set me in the parlor on the top shelf of a pretty, glass-front china cabinet that Fielden had built for her. I still loved Laura and knew she still loved me, because sometimes when she dusted me, she picked me up and kissed me. But I still felt lonely.

Laura was a busy homemaker now, cooking, cleaning and working in her vegetable garden. As she worked, I enjoyed listening to her sing hymns and folk songs. The couple was thrilled when they had two daughters, Ola and Flavia, then a son, Martin, then in two years, another son, Wilbur. Later two more little girls, Bessie and Daisy, were added to the family but, like the first two girls, they didn't care much for dolls. Fielden, a rice farmer and cattle rancher, worked hard to make a good living for this fast-growing family.

Laura and Baby Effie Pearl

Two years later, I heard another baby crying and Laura walked into the parlor with a little bundle in her arms. From my shelf in the china cabinet, I watched her unwrap the tiniest, reddest, little baby girl I had ever seen! Laura picked me up and said, "Daisy, meet Annabelle. Someday when you are older, I will let you play with her." The pretty brown-haired baby looked at me in wonder and reached out to touch my dress, causing Laura to smile proudly. Frau Anjabel had talked about humans being born as tiny babies, then becoming children and finally growing up into adults. Later, they marry and have their own babies and the cycle begins all over again.

Baby Daisy grew into a pretty little girl, who looked somewhat like her father. Laura had made her a sunbonnet, but like her mother when she had been a young girl, Daisy hardly ever wore it. To her parents' consternation, she was a "tomboy" and preferred to be outside climbing trees and riding horses with Martin and Wilbur rather than playing dolls, so I continued to sit on the shelf and watch the children grow as time passed by.

Three years later, another daughter, Effie Pearl, was born to Laura and her beloved Fielden. Little Effie looked much like Laura with black hair, big sea-green eyes, and a wide full mouth that smiled most of the time. I was glad to see that she liked dolls. One day, when Effie was six years old, Laura lifted me down from the china cabinet and dusted off my dress. She called Effie over and placed me in her eager arms. "Effie, I've saved my precious porcelain doll for a daughter who will love her and take very good care of her."

Effie nodded enthusiastically as Laura continued. "She is a very special doll that I have had since I was twelve years old. Now, I am giving Annabelle to you for your very own. Take good care of her." I was pleased when Effie, all smiles, hugged me close but I wondered if it was possible to love a second owner. Could I ever love her as much as I loved Laura?

The Stubbs' family was not at all wealthy, in fact, there never seemed to be enough money to go around for things the children needed. But their home seemed to always be filled with the children's laughter, music from Fielden's fiddle and Laura's singing, and often, the company of Grandmother Annie, visiting aunts, uncles, cousins and friends. Laura would often let the children make popcorn from corn they had grown in the field and shucked off the cob for a snack.

Sometimes, she and the girls would make fudge or taffy. Candy making was always an event the children loved. The children especially liked to make taffy and have "taffy pulls." After washing and buttering their hands, they would be given a heaping spoonful of the warm candy that had been cooked in a pot, to pull and twist. When the sweet, gooey taffy began to cool and turned a light golden color, it was ready to eat!

During the long summer evenings, while the children played, Laura often sat on the screened-in front porch in her rocking chair with her sewing basket and clothes in need of mending, while Fielden would sit beside her weaving his fishing nets from heavy string. They enjoyed watching their carefree youngsters swinging on the grapevines that hung down from the big trees in the front yard or playing tag. Sometimes, Fielden got the cane poles from the barn and the family would go fishing on the Old River dock in back of Grandmother Annie's house. On other evenings, they would take empty syrup buckets and go out into the field near the woods to pick juicy black-berries for pies. Of course, several cousins usually joined the fun. And so the years passed.

Time for School

After the last harvest in September, school would start and con-tinue until the end of April. Martin, Wilbur, Ola, Flavia, Bessie, Daisy, and Effie usually rode horses to The Cove's one-room schoolhouse. Three of the bigger kids and four of the little ones could fit on their two horses. All of the school children tethered their horses near the school-house in a grassy grove of trees that sat beside a little stream. On the first day of school, Miss Katie, the schoolteacher, would come out on the porch and ring the big bell. Then they all went inside and stood against the walls. Miss Katie assigned each one of the students to their desk. Each row of desks would be a different grade. Effie and Daisy were excited because they liked school and had been promoted to the second and fifth grade rows.

Martin and Wilbur, who didn't care for school as much as their sis-ters did, sat in the back with the older students who were sometimes reminded with a long switch to "mind their manners and pay atten-tion." Miss Katie taught all of them to add, subtract, multiply, and divide by ciphering numbers with chalk on little black slates. The stu-dents learned to read from the American School Reader and The Holy Bible. They all learned to spell from The Children's Speller and the older students memorized and recited passages from Our Great Nation's History.

Miss Katie Teaching School

Sometimes, Effie took me to school so she and her friends could play dolls at recess. I had many good times with sweet little Effie Pearl, but I always struggled with the guilty feeling that I did never love her as much as I loved Laura.

Martin and Wilbur's Terrible Trick

One fall evening, after the supper dishes were washed and dried, Bessie, Daisy and Effie asked Mother Laura if they could make some chocolate fudge. Their mother smiled and agreed, thinking that it was a good time to teach her two little girls another cooking lesson. Laura added another log to the fire in the wood stove, gave them aprons and brought out a stool for Effie to stand on while they were cooking. She put Bessie in charge since she was the oldest. Mother Laura let them take turns stirring the sugar and butter in the big, iron pot, already warming on the stove. Then, she pointed up to the shelf beside the wood stove and showed them where the bottle of vanilla was kept and left the room. Bessie had helped her before to make fudge, but she decided to let the girls do it by themselves this time.

"We add three caps of vanilla after the candy boils and thickens," Bessie, who enjoyed being the boss, tossed her hair and explained. "Then, we take the pot off the fire and beat it until it loses its shine. After that, we will pour the fudge out onto this cookie sheet and sprinkle pecans on top and the candy will be very good." The younger girls listened carefully to her.

Little Effie had not learned to read very well yet, so when she went to reach for the vanilla, big brothers Martin and Wilbur, who were standing nearby, switched the big brown bottle of vanilla with a similar bottle of Black Drought Cough Syrup that Mother Laura also kept upon the shelf. Pretending to help his sister, Martin reached up and handed the bottle to Effie. Bessie failed to notice as Daisy stirred and Effie poured three full caps of medicine into the candy, then replaced the cap and put the bottle back on the shelf.

He and Wilbur slinked out of the room, trying hard not to laugh at their prank and thinking what a great joke this was going to be. They ducked into the parlor and fell on the sofa laughing so hard they both rolled off onto the floor. They congratulated themselves on how easy it had been to fool their little sisters.

After supper that evening, Bessie cut their candy into squares and Daisy and Effie proudly brought it into the parlor to serve the family. Everyone took a piece, except Martin and Wilbur, and began to eat it. Suddenly they all started making faces and choking!

"Oh my!" Mother Laura finally declared. "Girls, what did you put into this fudge?"

Effie and Daisy both began to cry over their dismal failure, but Bessie, who had a quick mind and temper, stomped her foot and shouted at the boys. She had seen enough of their pranks to know they had done something to ruin the candy. Suddenly, Mother Laura recognized the taste— the licorice flavoring of Black Drought Cough Syrup. She took one look at the two red-faced boys and knew what had happened and Papa Fielden also knew. He grabbed both boys up by their arms and hauled them out to the barn for a good spanking, in spite of their wails and cries. The two younger girls quit crying and giggled with Bessie when they saw that, just like the fudge, justice was now being served.

That night, everyone ate the precious candy, including Martin and Wilbur, making faces after every bite, but continuing to eat because they so seldom had candy. After the children were all in bed, Laura giggled and said to Fielden, "At least, maybe our children won't have coughs for a while!" She and her husband laughed together very softly, so the youngsters wouldn't hear them.

* * * * *

As my family's life continued, it never occurred to me that my feelings of loving only Laura and not Effie were selfish on my part. Perhaps, we bring many problems upon ourselves by thinking only about our own feelings. I simply decided that, since I could not change the situation, I would do my very best to adjust to it. There was no way I could know that in less than a year, Effie, who loved me very much, would risk her very own life to save me.

Truly yours, Annabelle

The Bolivar Point Lighthouse

CHAPTER 12:

The Panther Sneaks Closer

7:00PM~~Galveston, Night of the Hurricane

Two hours later, the water had risen to four feet and, although the house was firmly set on four feet of solid concrete blocks with a cement foundation beneath, seawater had covered the big front porch and crept under the front door. Within the hour, two feet of water had completely covered the downstairs floor. Trying to salvage the furniture, the adults began grabbing whatever they could and hauling it upstairs.

"The water's never come up this far!" I heard Ben whisper to Daniel. They sat the writing desk down in a corner of the bedroom and he rubbed his bandaged brow. Daniel saw him stagger a little and stepped over to help him. Ben held up his hand and shook his head in refusal, then thought better and sat down. "Dan, I'm depending on you to be strong. This is a very bad hurricane. You are the second in command, but if I can't continue, *you must* take over." Daniel's brow furrowed as he nodded seriously, then headed back downstairs for more furniture.

Laura stood looking out of a small, east-side window toward the Galveston Ship Channel and Bolivar Point on the other side. The tall, black and white-striped lighthouse was standing stoically against the storm as it had for so many years. She took comfort in the fact that its light was still shining brightly, a beacon of hope to ships and sailors caught in a battle with the weather to get to land. It brought to mind a hymn about a lighthouse that she had often sung in their small Cove Community Church. Never before had she truly grasped the meaning so clearly as she did tonight. She bowed her head and prayed silently to the Lord for protection. She would later learn that a hundred and twenty-five people had made their way to the shelter and safety of the Bolivar Lighthouse.

"Is this part of our dress-up game?" asked Daisy, Donnie and Effie. They jumped up and down on Henrietta's big bed, totally unaware of the rising water.

"You Bet!" Daniel answered. He carried in the big parlor chair. "And we are going to need nice furniture for it." Then, he put on a big grin for the girls.

Ben agonized over not being able to get his family off the island and to the safety of The Cove. Both Henrietta and Laura tried to comfort him, explaining that there had been no warning until this afternoon and that he had no way of knowing. Everyone had thought it was simply a summer storm.

"It's my duty to keep you all safe." He beat his fist on his knee. "I should have realized that this was a hurricane!"

Henrietta would have none of it and assured him that he was a smart, responsible husband and father. She told him how the weatherman, Isaac Cline, had gone back and forth on the beach in his buggy, begging people to leave. Most of them, however, had laughed and refused to listen to his warnings.

Ben shook his head and went back down for kitchen chairs. "Pa made his living from the sea and Daniel and I do the same. We will deal with the sea now." With resolution in his eyes, he added, "This strong, old house has been through many storms and several hurricanes. With God's help, we will get through this one!" Meanwhile, the monster storm roared closer and faster toward the helpless island.

Laura put some more quilts down on the bedroom floor. They had now grown used to the idea that they were in the midst of a hurricane, but still had no idea how terrible it was going to be. The girls and little Don snuggled down into the covers, giggling and tickling one another.

"How about a story, Mama?" Daisy asked. All eyes and ears turned toward Laura and the children forgot about the storm for a few blissful moments as she began. Now I will relate it to you:

The Chocolate Cake Theft—December, 1899

By December, the crops had all been harvested and sold and cattle branding was done. Grandmother Annie had invited the entire family to come to her home for a big Christmas reunion. Laura and her sisters met at Mother Annie's house the week before the gathering to plan the holiday festivities for their big family.

Fielden was sitting in the parlor reading the newspaper he had brought home from Barber's Hill when Laura walked in with a twinkle in her eyes and humming a Christmas carol. 'What have you ladies been up to?' he asked looking up.

'Oh, only the best party ever had in The Cove!' replied Laura, brimming over with excitement to tell Fielden about all the plans they had made.

She hung her bonnet and shawl on the pegs by the door and sat down on the sofa beside him. I became excited, too, as I sat on my parlor shelf and listened. They had decided to have a hayride for the young people. Fielden would chop down a big pine tree and everyone would help decorate it. They had even divided up the dishes that each family would prepare and bring. Laura laughed as she related how Mother Annie had more fun than anyone planning the party.

The next morning, after she got the children off to school, Laura sent Fielden out to pick up pecans from under their trees. She assigned him the task of shelling them while she went out to the hen house to gather eggs. Afterward, Fielden went out to the backyard wood pile and chopped some more wood. He brought a big armful of logs into the parlor, unloaded it by the fireplace and added a few of them to the fire to ward off the chill. At last, Fielden sat down in his favorite chair before the warm, crackling flames and enjoyed the warmth. Then he began cracking and filling a bowl with the rich, brown nuts he had brought in.

Laura washed her hands and rolled out pie dough and divided it into three balls of dough, enough for three big pies. As soon as Fielden had shelled the pecans, she mixed them with syrup and poured the filling into pie shells and popped them into the wood stove's oven. It wasn't long before three brown, steaming, pecan pies came out. Next, she sifted flour, cocoa and baking soda over butter and sugar in a big bowl and added fresh buttermilk and eggs. The final result was a big, beautiful chocolate cake that she covered with thick chocolate icing and sprinkled with chopped pecans. Fielden, drawn into the kitchen by the delicious smells, stood eyeing the beautiful cake.

'Don't you dare!' warned Laura, laughing. 'These pies and cake are for the party Saturday.' She handed him a cup of hot coffee and some cookies as she shooed him with her apron back to his chair beside the fireplace. Then she started supper.

By the time the children came home from school, Laura had securely locked the cake and pies in the pantry. She knew that the desserts would be devoured if they were discovered and there would be nothing left to take to Mother Annie's party. Then she hung the key in its secret place behind the wood box next to the stove.

Fielden always said that their boys had a sense of smell that rivaled hound dogs, but no one realized that they had smelled the chocolate cake, locked away in the pantry, as soon as they had come in from school that evening. The two, mischievous youngsters waited until everyone was asleep, then slipped quietly out of bed. I heard them as they tiptoed past our bedroom and into the kitchen.

Laura didn't realize that Wilbur knew where she kept the pantry key. He had seen the tiny gleam behind the wood box one evening when he brought in the wood and dumped it into the wood box. Tonight, he reached over the wood box, felt for the key's hanger and carefully lifted the key off. In a few moments, I heard them as they unlocked and opened the pantry door. For the longest time, the house was very quiet. Suddenly, I heard the pantry door close and the key turn again. The boys slipped back to their bedroom, thinking their mother would be none the wiser and would believe that mice had gotten into the cake.

The next morning, when Laura unlocked the pantry and stepped inside to get pancake flour, she stopped short in her tracks and stared at the plate where her beautiful chocolate cake had been. There were only several broken pieces of cake lying on the plate with icing smeared around. Sure that the mischievous boys did the deed, she started to go out and get a switch, but thought for a moment and decided to say nothing. Instead she made a big stack of sweet buttermilk pancakes. When the children came into the kitchen for breakfast, she fixed their plates with pancakes and poured the sweet, home-made cane syrup over them. 'Now, I want you to clean your plates this morning. It is cold out and you need a good, hardy breakfast before going to school.'

Ola, Flavia, Bessie, Daisy and Effie all eagerly replied, 'Yes, Ma'am!' They quickly dove into their pancakes, as did their little brother, Donnie. Then she handed the boys their plates, stacked high with the biggest pancakes and swimming in cane syrup. Martin and Wilbur looked sheepishly at each other, then at the huge amounts of food.

Begrudgingly, they began to eat. It wasn't long before they slowed down and were about to quit until Laura told them firmly to clean their plates before getting up. By the time they finished their last bite, their faces *were white and they had stomach aches. Both boys begged to stay home, but she and Fielden would hear none of it and sent them off to school along with their sisters.*

After they left, I could hear Laura and Fielden laughing for a long time as she told him the story. He went back to shelling pecans again while she mixed up another cake and also a big batch of teacakes for the party. It was quite a while before the boys wanted any more chocolate cake, and I do believe that was the last time they slipped into the pantry.

The adults smiled wearily when they noticed that the children had drifted off to sleep. At last they, too, had a chance to rest for a little while.

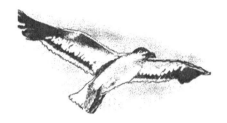

CHAPTER 13:

Night in the Attic

9:00P.M.~~Galveston, Night of the Hurricane

The women were unaware that the salt water silently filled the ten-foot-high first story of the big house, but Ben was watching the water rise from the attic window and thinking about what he must do if it kept getting worse. The night was pitch-black outside and he felt utterly alone except for the terrible howling of the wind, the beating rain and faraway crashes. "God help us and all the others on this island. Please show me what to do," he muttered to himself. Suddenly, he realized what action he must take to save their lives. He turned and bounded down to the second-floor bedroom.

"Wake up!" he whispered huskily, shaking Henrietta's shoulder. "We have to get up to the attic!" Daniel woke up instantly and picked up little Effie, who was holding me in her arms. The women grabbed Daisy and Baby Don. They all hurried up the narrow stairs to the third floor attic. In a few moments, Henrietta, Ben and Daniel ran back down the stairs while Laura stayed in the attic with the children. She lit a hurricane lamp and put blankets around them. Effie sat me down and moved under a blanket with her sister, Daisy, and little Donnie. Quickly, the raincoats, food, water, ropes, and tools that had been brought up to the second floor were retrieved and rushed up to the attic. Henrietta also grabbed quilts and pillows from the floor. Soon everyone was in the third floor attic, dry and safe for the moment.

Just then, the ferocious wind blew the shutters off the big attic window overlooking the Galveston Bay. "Children, stay under the quilts!" Ben shouted. Sleepy Effie tossed me in a nearby corner and dove under the quilts with the others. "The rest of you, help me push this big, old armoire in front of the window facing the bay." They all grabbed hold of the huge piece of old furniture and shoved with all their might. Slowly, they began to move it and, after a few minutes, it was in place blocking the window. A minute later, the glass shattered and, to our relief, fell harmlessly in back of the heavy armoire storage chest.

During that fearful night, the three suspicious children, now awake again, lay under the blankets on the attic floor. The two girls, being older, knew that something was definitely wrong. Only little Donnie was still under the impression that they were playing a game. Twelve year-old Daisy saw the worry on her mother and Aunt Henrietta's faces and knew that they were trying to hide it from her, Effie and Donnie. "Aunt Henrietta, will you tell us a story this time?" she asked innocently, masking the fear in her own voice. I could tell that this young lady was, tonight, making great strides toward maturity.

"Well, all right, let's see." Henrietta stuttered, trying to think of an event that would take their minds off the terror of this night. "Oh, I know! How about last Christmas at Mother Annie's house? Laura, you can fill in the gaps for me, okay?"

Laura nodded eagerly and all three children agreed that last Christmas would make a perfect story, so Henrietta began.

1899~~Christmas in The Cove

I love Christmas! It is a time of faith, peace, love, and celebration. Most of all, it is a time of joy!" It seems that things in the human world are always changing. As quickly as you get used to one situation, it changes to another. Perhaps one day I will get used to change. The time would come sooner than I expected, but for now, I shall relate to you the story that Henrietta told the children that night in the attic.

Your friend, Annabelle

*****

The Prettiest Tree~~Christmas Eve

"Early in the morning of Christmas Eve, Fielden hitched the horses up to the wagon and called the boys to go with him to the woods to look for a Christmas tree.

"Laura interjected, 'We're gonna bring back the prettiest tree in the woods! Y'all be ready to go to Grandmother Annie's when we get back,' called Martin, as Pa whistled and the horses trotted away.' Then she nodded for Henrietta to continue.

"Then Henrietta continued, making up parts she didn't know. 'While they were gone, Laura set all their packed bags by the door, then let Bessie and Flavia pop some of her shucked corn in the fireplace and the girls began making popcorn strings for the tree. As they worked, they sang Christmas carols. It wasn't long before they heard the horses' bells jingling. Effie grabbed me and she, Bessie, Flavia, Daisy and Mother Laura all ran outside to see the biggest, most perfect tree they had ever seen.

"'It's so big and beautiful!' Bessie shouted as she touched the fragrant branches.

"'I found it and Wilbur chopped it down,' Martin announced, grinning from ear to ear, and as proud as punch.

"'Boys, get our bags. Girls, hop up here in the wagon and we will all take this tree and ourselves on over to Mother Annie's.' Fielden called and beckoned to the girls and Laura. She hurried back into the house to retrieve the popcorn strings the girls had just made, show Martin and Wilbur where the bags were and grab little Donnie by the hand.

"'Go to Gwanma's, go Gwanma's house!' He clapped his chubby hands and grinned as he repeated himself over and over.

"Mother Annie heard the commotion and singing as they pulled up in her yard and came outside. She was very excited to get such a nice tree, but wondered if they could get it through the door! Everyone pushed and pulled and finally drug the tree into the house and set it up. Indeed, it was a beautiful tree and smelled of strong, sweet pine needles. All of the sisters pulled their popcorn strings out of their apron pockets and began hanging decorations while little Donnie sat down and began eating the one Laura had made for him."

"How am I doing?" Henrietta looked questioningly at Laura.

Laura nodded and whispered, "Fine." So Henrietta continued.

"Soon the big pine tree looked like a beautiful Christmas tree, indeed!

"Other members of the Tilton family soon began to arrive for the big 'get together' and, by noon, the old Tilton homestead was filled with laughter and squeals of children.

"Excitement was in the air as all of Laura's sisters and brothers and their families filled the old house to bursting by that afternoon. Some had brought their families in wagons from as far away as Houston and others came on horseback from the nearby town of Barbers Hill and The Cove area. Even Ben and Henrietta and their children and grand-children had sailed in from Galveston. Their daughters, Rachel, Julia and Nora were grown up and married but their only son, Dan, who was engaged, still lived at home and worked with Ben in the hauling business.

(Effie was so excited about the Christmas celebration that she had laid me down on Grandmother Annie's kitchen table, but Laura wisely picked me up and placed me high up on the parlor mantle. From that wonderful vantage point, I could see the beautiful Christmas tree, everyone in the parlor, and all the way into the kitchen. I was even able to peek through the windows at the children playing outside. She straightened my dress, smiled, and turned back toward the kitchen.)

"Annie Tilton was thrilled that all of her children and their families were here and enjoyed their laughter and much talk. Children ran across the yard playing tag while the women discussed the newest dress patterns and recipes of dishes they had brought into the big kitchen and the men sat in the parlor talking about their latest hunting and fishing adventures.

The Prettiest Tree in the Woods

"That night, all of the cousins slept on pallets made of fluffy, home-made quilts, the girls in the parlor and the boys in the study. They all whispered and giggled in anticipation of Christmas morning until Father yelled down the stairs for the house to get quiet if they wanted Santa Claus to come. Effie watched the soft moonlight dance over the beautiful tree and its shiny glass balls and thought it was the most beautiful sight she had ever seen. Finally, the children closed their eyes and drifted off to sleep. The End."

Henrietta finished the story and smiled when she noticed that the children were asleep. So she closed her eyes too.

* * * * *

9:30P.M.~~Galveston, Night of the Hurricane

Meanwhile, Ben stood at the attic entrance and watched the water creep over the second floor stairs. I was sure he wondered how much more water pressure the house could take before giving way. Since dolls do not sleep, I could only watch Ben's lined face in the flickering lamplight. Even though this was not his fault, he had heaped all of the guilt upon himself. That was his way. Ben was a fine man and a good father to his children and I respected him a great deal. He was staunch, brave and demanding but, inside, he had a big, loving heart. I thought that his father, Charles Tilton, must have been somewhat like him.

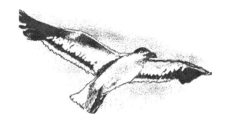

CHAPTER 14:

Dangerous Escape

Effie had forgotten about me and left me lying in the attic corner. I knew that this was probably going to be the end of my life, but I wasn't afraid because I had already had a wonderful, long life and had been loved by two owners! All I hoped and prayed for was for Laura, Effie, and the rest of my family to be saved.

Yours truly, Annabelle

10:00PM.~~Galveston, Night of the Hurricane

"Daniel, come with me," Ben called. "We are going back down to the bedroom to take the bed apart!" he told his son. Daniel jumped up and obeyed without a word, but everyone looked at each other, wondering if his father had lost his mind.

Both men rummaged and found some tools in an attic storage barrel, then rushed downstairs to Henrietta and Ben's bedroom, where the floor was already covered in two feet of water. Laura and Henrietta stationed themselves on the stairs to help. Soon they were dragging the massive carved oak headboard, which reached almost to the ceiling, into the attic. Afterward, the men lugged the big footboard, which was only slightly smaller, up the stairs as the two women pulled it into the attic.

Daniel finally asked the question, "Father, what are we going to do with this bed?"

Ben pulled him over toward the corner where I lay, and spoke quietly so that the others would not hear. "This is the worst hurricane that I can ever remember. I fear that the house may be coming off its foundation. We have to escape or we could be trapped and washed out to sea," I heard Ben say quietly. A shiver of terror for my family went through me.

Daniel started to respond but Ben whispered frantically, "Stop! Be still! Do you feel that?" Daniel's eyes grew big and fear rose in his throat as he felt the floor swaying ever so slightly.

Laura and Henrietta, now wide-awake, also felt it and stood frozen in terror. They would have screamed, but knew they must not frighten the children. In the flickering lamplight, I could see the terrible fear on their faces.

"Listen to me!" Ben had a plan and conveyed it to everyone. "Henrietta and Laura, I need you to be brave and do exactly as I say." The two women nodded frantically.

"When the calm eye of the hurricane reaches us, Daniel and I will ease the big headboard out through the bay window and onto the roof then secure Henrietta and Baby Don to it. Next, we'll slide the footboard out and lash Laura and the girls to it. Laura started to interrupt at hearing that she would not have her baby with her, but Ben held his hand up to stop her. Luckily, we keep a lot of old rope up here in the attic. Laura, we'll tie you to the left side of the headboard and Dan on the right side with your girls in between both of you. I'll link myself to the footboard with ropes and help Henrietta hold on to little Don, because I'm strong enough to hold him. I'll push us off the roof into the water, as soon as everyone is secured to the bed boards."

Everyone was too stunned to react to Ben's dangerous plan. They stood staring at him, as he skillfully cut and wrapped ropes around the headboard and the footboard. He used sailors' square knots that his father had taught him so that they would not come loose, even when wet. Could such a dangerous escape plan really work? If it didn't, they would all surely die. I decided to try praying, too, although I never had.

Somehow, I remembered Frau Anjabel Schneider's happy voice singing church songs and prayers, so I tried them.

Henrietta was the first to notice that the wind had stopped blowing. The hurricane had stalled as though catching its breath for a final massive assault. "We're in the eye of the hurricane," she whispered.

"We have to work quickly before the other side of the hurricane hits," Ben said. He fished an old shovel out of a barrel of broken tools and rope and hacked at the vertical beam, which was standing in the center of the bay window, until it broke.

Meanwhile, Daniel chopped at the heavy wooden window frame to widen the opening. He and Ben then secured several long ropes from inside the attic and attached them to the headboard and footboard. They eased the bed boards through the big window and onto the steep roof and then, tying the ends of the ropes to themselves, climbed out onto the wet roof.

Laura helped Henrietta tie ropes around each of the frightened girls. Then, one at a time, they, too, climbed out onto the roof. Surprisingly, Donnie wasn't scared at all, thinking this was a game. A thin sliver of moonlight shined down through the hurricane's eye and dead calm began. The rain stopped, helping the family find footing on the slick shingles.

Ben guided Henrietta, little Don, and Laura down to the massive bed boards. He and Daniel carefully edged Daisy and Effie down the sloping roof, next. "It's a good thing that my father made these bed boards so big and that he used good, heavy oak. I'm sure they will hold all of us up!" he said, trying to calm his wife, daughter and the children. They nodded just before he covered them with a piece of canvas, but he wasn't sure if they heard him or were just responding out of shock.

Laura swallowed her fear and, holding Daisy, pulled her onto the headboard and began securing her with the ropes. Then, Daniel handed off Effie to her, and began securing her beside Daisy. The girls were sniffling, so Dan ordered them to stop crying. Surprised at his

Ben & Daniel hold the ropes

firmness, they hushed. "We will be brave because we are grandchildren of a brave pirate," he said. He hoped they didn't hear the distant crashes of buildings and screams.

As I lay alone in the dim attic corner, I was not afraid but, rather, I was relieved that they had escaped the crumbling house. "Thank you, God, for getting my family out of this house. Good-bye, my Laura and my little Effie Pearl," I called silently. "May you have a safe journey and live through this terrible hurricane." I knew I had seen the last of my dear American frontier family but, until now, I had not realized how much I loved Effie. I now saw how self-centered I had been to think I could not love this little girl who adored me.

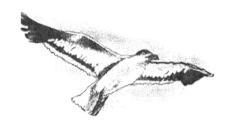

CHAPTER 15:

Effie Risks Her Life

I'm learning about this strange emotion that humans call 'love'. You can love someone so much that your heart feels so full that it might burst with happiness. You think that there is no room at all left inside of it to love anyone else. But I see now that when a new love comes into your life, suddenly your heart grows big enough for both.

Most kindly yours, Annabelle

* * * * *

11:00PM.~~Night of the Hurricane

Suddenly, Effie shrieked. "Ma, I left Annabelle in the corner! We have to save her, too!" Before Dan could grab her, the determined, stubborn girl, so much like her mother, wiggled free of the ropes and bolted back up the slick roof. She quickly went through the bay window to search the attic corner where she had left me. Oh, how I wished that she would have just forgotten about me because, at that moment, the big house began to groan and sway again.

"Effie, come back!" Laura screamed. She also struggled free and began crawling back up the wet wooden shingle roof with Daniel close behind her. Just then, Effie reappeared at the window, waving me like a banner, then she climbed back out onto the roof again.

Laura Tries to Save Effie

Daisy, already tied fast to the headboard, watched her little sister from under the oilcloth in horror. "Hurry, Effie! Come On!" she yelled through the semi-darkness. Just then, the wind from the backside of the hurricane hit the damaged, old, window frame. It slammed down, catching me under it, halfway in and halfway out. Laura was trying to reach her daughter, but Effie, blinded by the stinging rain that had begun again, was losing her foothold as she tried unsuccessfully to pull me loose.

Henrietta screamed, "Effie, leave the doll! Slide down to your mother!" Daisy yelled, "Leave that stupid doll, Effie, and come on, please!"

Henrietta tried a different tactic. "Effie, we'll buy you another doll!" But their cries fell on deaf ears because Effie had made up her mind to rescue her precious Annabelle because she loved her.

"Oh, God, don't let her die. Help her, please." Henrietta prayed aloud.

Ben and Daniel could only watch in terror as they struggled to hold the footboard and headboard steady near the roof's edge. Despite their strength, the bed boards began to slide slowly and dangerously over to the edge. The rain began coming down in sheets again, but determined to free me, Effie kept struggling with the window frame. Suddenly, a gust of whirling wind caused her to lose both her foothold and her balance. She was suspended in the air like a kite, with only one of her hands gripping the window ledge. Laura screamed and stretched out her arm, but couldn't quite reach her precious daughter. Everyone froze in horror, expecting Effie to tumble toward the swirling water any second.

I realized that this was a life or death situation, as humans call it, and knew that I must break the doll's code of silence once more. I had spoken softly to Laura long ago, and now, for the second time in my life, I spoke again. Yelling as loudly as I could and hoping Effie could hear me, I called, "Effie, grab onto me! I will hold you!"

"All right!" she cried in complete trust, grabbing hold of my porcelain legs, which were sticking out from under the frame. Clutching my legs with both hands, she now frantically scraped the roof with the toes of her shoes, trying to gain a foothold on the wet shingles.

Unexpectedly, I felt one of my porcelain legs crack and then break off just below the knee! Horrified, Effie watched as it plummeted down the roof, as though in slow motion, and plunged into the raging, black water, but she doggedly held on to my other leg and grabbed my body with her free hand. The next instant, Laura reached her side. "Mama, Annabelle saved me! She told me what to do! We have to get her free and save her! She's my best friend!"

Laura nodded, in that instant remembering a time long ago when Annabelle had been her best friend. "Did Annabelle really speak to Effie just as she did to me many years ago?" The question whirled through Laura's mind as she clutched Effie with one arm and struggled with the other one to push the wooden window frame up. She pressed against it with all her strength, ignoring the pieces of glass sticking into her hands. Suddenly the frame shot upward just high enough to dislodge me. The determined little girl ripped me free, pulled me into her arms, and tucked me safely down inside the top of her apron.

Laura grabbed her tightly and began to work her way down the sloping roof. She tried to ignore the shingles that were now flying through the air at a high speed.

A huge gust of wind toppled the flickering lamp, left in the attic, onto the floor. It shattered and kerosene spilled over the floor, instantly causing a wild blaze that spread throughout the room in just seconds. Laura knew they had to get off the roof quickly.

"Effie, we have to get down to the raft. Lie flat on your stomach and hold on to me!" yelled Laura. The raging fire was now driven by the wind onto the roof amidst great hisses and crackles as the rain hit it and illuminated the roof enough so that they could see.

Effie had now used up all of her courage and was terrified to move. Holding her daughter tightly, Laura tried to give her the courage she needed. "Effie, you can do this. You are a strong, brave pioneer girl! You can do it for Papa and me!" Effie finally nodded weakly. Slowly and steadily, they began sliding down the steep, wet roof.

"Hurry, the eye of the hurricane has passed over!" Ben called over the roar of the increasingly violent wind. He and Daniel tied the last ropes linking the headboard and footboard together and, at the same time, tried to keep them from slipping off the roof's edge. Boards and other objects were now being hurled through the air. "We can't hold on much longer!"

At last, Daniel caught hold of Laura and Effie and quickly lashed both of them next to little Daisy onto the headboard. Then, he linked the end of the long rope around his waist so he could swim and hang on. "We're ready!" he cried. It took all of Ben and Dan's strength to push the headboard and footboard off the roof. The heavy bed boards fell six feet through the darkness and hit the surging waves, dipped perilously below the water, choking its passengers, but popping back to the surface over and over. At last, the men jumped into the blackness with only two ropes linking them to the bed boards.

The family watched as the entire top of their home went up in flames and with a gigantic death knell, toppled over and crashed into the sea. Suddenly, they were plunged into total darkness and the merciless jaws of this savage panther. Brick buildings were sliding into the sea all around and hundreds of people were screaming for help that could not come.

A mother and her little girl floated past Ben on a door. As they bumped into the raft, she cried tearfully, "Save my baby girl, please, please!" He reached out to her and managed to touch the baby's tiny fingers. Just then, another wave washed over and the mother and baby both disappeared beneath the churning water. He wept silently for them and for everyone meeting a watery death that night. He knew he would never forget the anguish.

* * * * *

12:00 Midnight--Night of the Hurricane

Through the last hours of darkness and into the early dawn of that long, horrible Galveston Hurricane of 1900, the entire family, in terror and shock, clung tightly under the ropes and to the wooden bed boards that had now become their links to life. The nightmares they thought they were having had become quite real. "Mama," Donnie wailed until he had no more strength left. Daisy screamed hysterically, "I'm scared and cold! The ropes are cutting into me!"

"Be brave, Daisy!" urged Effie. "We have to do this for Mama and Papa and for our whole family. We have to live! Scoot closer to me so we will be warmer." My doll's heart went out to the young girls, both of whom I had come to love. Surely this horror would end soon.

CHAPTER 16:

Terrifying Night in the Sea

2:00A.M.~~Night of the Hurricane

Both wooden rafts, loaded with the terrified passengers, lurched beneath the cold, dark waves every few minutes. They threatened to drag the helpless victims to the bottom but then, they would pop back up to the surface. The wind raged in every direction while huge waves washed over them. Defenseless, they could only cough up seawater, cry and brace themselves for the next horrible moment. Ben held Laura's little boy tightly between him and Henrietta and whenever their raft threatened to dive under a wave, he held the baby's nose and mouth. Little Don screamed at first but was finally reduced to whimpers. Effie and Daisy, wedged between Laura and Daniel, quickly learned to take a deep breath and hold it when they felt their raft tilting downward. All the while, Daniel kept his arm around Effie as Laura gripped Daisy tightly.

Broken tree limbs, lumber and unidentified objects flew overhead continually, some hitting them then bouncing into the water. A board hit Laura squarely in the back, knocking her unconscious for a few moments. When she finally was able to catch her breath, she realized that she was badly cut but she didn't cry out. She wept and gripped Daisy and Effie even tighter. Her daughters were battered and bruised and sobbed intermittently.

Henrietta endured a broken arm, but did not complain. Instead, she cried aloud in prayer as she held tightly onto Donnie with the other arm and Ben encircled both of them with his big, strong arm. Ben and Daniel, who had stayed afloat by clinging to the bedposts, had finally managed to grope their way aboard, squeeze under the wet ropes and tie themselves on the makeshift rafts with loose, hanging ropes. Now they used most of their strength holding the others on the bed boards. The night seemed agonizingly long as though it would never end.

Raft Caught in Bushes

Secured together, the strange rafts were all that stood between the family and certain death. Everyone was cold and soaked by the deluge of rain and the angry, pounding waves but, at least, they were still alive. "How much longer can we survive?" They all wondered silently. Quietly, Effie reached down into her apron top with one hand and stroked my porcelain head. It would have been a heart wrenching site to see the soaked, exhausted little group if, indeed, anyone could have seen them during this dark night.

My doll's heart was breaking for my brave family. They were fighting hard but were losing strength. I wondered how long they could continue. It seems that humans cannot endure such terrible ordeals.

Yours, Annabelle

* * * * *

3:00A.M~~Night of the Hurricane

At last the waves and wind began to diminish. "Ooh, Mama, I'm sooo sick at my stomach!" whispered Effie. They had swallowed salt water almost every time a wave had swept over them.

Daniel and Laura could not see Ben and Henrietta's raft in the total darkness, but knew by the taunt rope that it was still attached. They realized that they needed to get the girls' minds off the lurching rafts and the wet ropes that were by now cutting into their skin.

Daniel thought of several jokes and told them to the girls between bursts of wind. Then Laura remembered an incident that had happened last year. "Girls, I have another story for you," she said. For the next half hour she managed, though I know not how, through cracked and bleeding lips, to hold their attention with the rest of the Christmas story from last December.

* * * * *

1899~~Christmas Morning at Grandmother Annie Tilton's

"Daisy and her cousin, Janie, sat up on their palette and said at the same time, 'It's Christmas. Everybody wake up!' Sleepy heads began to bob up from their pillows and all of the children jumped up and ran to the big Christmas tree.

"Instantly, they all chorused, 'Santa came!' There under the big pine tree, was a rag doll and a set of jacks for each girl, and a slingshot and a pair of stilts for each boy. There was even a big box filled with candy canes, nuts, and apples and oranges for all of them! They whooped and hollered, then quickly got dressed and ran outside to play with their new toys. Mother Annie gave the older children silver dollars, a beautiful cameo pin to each of her daughters and daughters-in-law, and hand-knitted mittens to her sons and sons-in-law.

* * * * *

"As usual on Christmas morning, no breakfast was served except for milk and cookies, then the children were quickly shooed outdoors. The women spent the morning in Mother Annie's spacious kitchen, cooking, visiting and laughing. The wonderful smells of the Christmas turkeys and stuffing baking in the big wood stove soon mingled with pots of endless coffee, fruit cider and hot chocolate. The sideboards were loaded with desserts: pecan, apple and mincemeat pies, cookies, fruitcakes, cream cakes, bread pudding, fruit salads, buttermilk pralines, divinity and fudge. And of course, everyone sampled the goodies from time to time!

"As a surprise, Ben and his brothers went down to the dock and unloaded a brand new foot-treadle sewing machine off of his schooner. They brought it into the house and presented it to Mother Annie as a Christmas surprise. She was overjoyed as she rubbed the black finish of the machine softly. 'It's from all of us," said her oldest son. Then, not wanting her to think he had spent an extravagant amount of money, Ben added, 'I got it for a good price from an English ship captain. He said it can sew a stitch every second!'

The women gasped in amazement because they sewed everything by hand and it took a long time to make even the simplest garment. They had heard of the new-fangled sewing machines, built by Mr. Singer, but no one had ever actually seen one. Mother Annie liked to make clothes for her grandchildren, so this was the perfect gift. She did something rare—she hugged everyone. Though the old lady strongly denied it later, some claimed to have seen her wipe tears away from her eyes with the corner of her new Christmas apron.

"Later in the parlor, the men discussed hunting, the weather and then hurricanes, as usual. Mother Annie stuck her head out from the kitchen and noticed some worried expressions on the women's faces. Mother Annie shook her finger and said, 'Now Ben, you're upsetting the women. No more talk about hurricanes! The Good Book says that we have enough troubles for today without borrowing any from tomorrow.'

"'You are right. I'm sorry,' Ben apologized, taking a puff of his pipe. 'But it is good if we can work with nature and not against it. We must never take the sea for granted.' All of the men nodded. Children ran in just then and the conversation came to a halt.

"Finally, the long-awaited call came: 'Everyone, wash up! The turkeys and hams are done so the meal will be ready in a few minutes!' announced Mother Annie loudly as she rang the dinner bell. All of the women helped dish up the food and set the big oak table for the grown-ups and the smaller tables for the children. As was the custom in those days, adults were served first and the children waited until last.

"'Mmm! I'm starving!' exclaimed the ever-hungry Daniel loudly. Everyone laughed and instantly forgot the subject of hurricanes. When they all sat down at the tables, Ben read the Christmas story from the Bible and his son-in-law, Rachel's husband, Harvey, gave thanks for the food and the wonderful season.

Late that afternoon after the dishes were all washed and food was put away, the family members began to say their "goodbyes." They hugged one another and Mother Annie. The men got their horses out of the corral and began hitching up their wagons to head back to their homes. Ben stood at the helm of *Black Jack II*, steering away from the dock and waving over his shoulder with his other hand. "This was the finest Christmas ever! Merry Christmas, Ma!" He called to the smiling, gray-haired lady, who stood as straight and tall as she always had. Ben's family waved to her and the rest of the family members until their boat sailed around Old River's bend and out of sight. What a wonderful Christmas it had been!

* * * * *

4:00 AM~~Galveston, Night of the Hurricane

Daniel looked at the two soaked girls between Laura and him. "Shhh," he whispered. They have finally fallen into a fitful sleep. Laura shut her eyes for a moment and thought of her home. She whispered that she hoped Mother Annie, her beloved Fielden and her two precious, mischievous boys at their home were all right. She was thankful because she knew they weren't yet aware that a killer hurricane had washed over the island.

She resumed her vigil of watching and holding her daughters tightly again. It was quieter now and the screams in the distance had finally stopped but they still whirled about in her mind.

I thought of home, too, just as Laura had, and I suddenly realized that Galveston, my first home, no longer held first place in my heart as it always had. My *home* now was Laura and Fielden Stubbs and their children's home. Home was where Effie lived. How silly I had been to long for the home in Galveston. A house could not be your home unless the ones you cared about the most were there. Now I knew that I really loved little Effie.

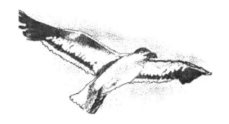

CHAPTER 17:

Dawning of a New Day

Just as a new day and a new beginning dawned in Galveston after the terrible hurricane, a new day and new beginning dawned for me. You may think that you can only love one person. Then someone new comes into your life and somehow your heart grows, keeping the old love while making room for the new. I am glad that I have realized that I CAN love Effie as much as I love Laura. And I now think that I can love each future generation of my little owners.

Yours truly, Annabelle

* * * * *

5:00AM~~Early Morning after the Hurricane

For the rest of that night the family floated in the darkness while the rafts rocked up and down but not quite so high. The debris that had so violently been flung through air now floated by, often bumping into them, and the ropes that had bound them so tightly were now loose. The adults dared not sleep because they still had to hold on to the children. They knew if they eased their watch, one of them might slip through the wet ropes.

Half asleep, Laura's tired mind drifted to thoughts of the warm raincoats they had left behind in the attic. Something abruptly bumped hard against the raft, wrenching her out of the dream. She stretched her free hand out into the darkness and felt shreds of a dress sleeve and a woman's arm. In her grogginess, she grabbed the woman and whispered,

"Here, let me help you. We have room for one more." Laura, still dazed, continued to hold on to the still figure. She asked, "Are you all right? You are so…." The word *cold* never passed her lips because she suddenly realized that this poor woman was not alive. She was now suddenly and completely alert and recoiled her hand in horror. She wanted to scream and scream, but knew that she couldn't because of the children. She could only cover her mouth, cry for this person, and wonder how many others had died that night.

Then, with a gasp of sorrow, she began to pray again, "Dear Jesus," as she silently wept.

At last, a calmness enveloped her being and she realized that she had to trust God with their lives because they had absolutely no power to save themselves. With that realization, she finally fell into a light sleep.

The wind slowly quieted down and the rain finally subsided. The girls who had slept only fitfully off and on, were now sound asleep. When Laura awoke, she numbly wondered what would have happened to Effie if she had not held on to Annabelle. What if Annabelle really had called to Effie? The only answer was that it had been a miracle if it really happened. But all that mattered now was that her precious daughter's life had been saved. Laura knew that she would always keep Annabelle as a treasured member of their family.

Ben was frantically hoping for a place to tie the rafts. The hurricane was no longer life-threatening but an equally large threat now loomed—that of being pulled out to sea in the fast, receding water. From inside Effie's apron, I felt a sudden lurch as the headboard and footboard bumped into something. I could tell that we had become entangled in some bushes or debris.

"Swim and tie on to the bushes!" cried Ben to Daniel. They both jumped into the water and wrapped the hanging ropes around some of the limbs as best they could. Then Ben yelled back to find out if every-one was all right. They were cold, bruised, bleeding and hurting but were all alive. Laura called to Henrietta to see how Baby Don was and Henrietta answered that he was sound asleep in her arms. Laura cried but it was from thankfulness, this time. They all had survived and were alive and safe.

5:30A.M.~~Terror in the Undertow

Suddenly, Henrietta heard a loud noise—the sounds of a huge wave, a heavy bump, and a gasp all at the same time. Thinking that she was only hearing the wind and water, she called Ben in her tired, weak voice. "Ben, did you hear that sound? What was it?" Perhaps her exhausted mind was playing tricks on her. She called again but there was no answer from her husband. Alarm rose in her chest and crawled up into her parched throat. Something was not right. Again, she called, but this time it was to Daniel. "Daniel, is Ben still with you in the water?"

Above the wind, she heard her son answering, as though from a distance. "No, Mom, he's swimming back to your raft," he called assuredly. "Give him a minute then pull on his rope."

Obeying her son, Henrietta waited and counted the seconds. Fear built as each one passed. Finally, she could wait no longer, so she pulled the rope that Ben had tied around himself. She pulled and pulled, wait-ing for the tautness of his body to stretch it tightly. One more pull and the end of the frayed rope popped up onto the raft with the loop where Ben's body should be, limp and empty. Henrietta stared in disbelief at the lifeline in her hand. Where was her big, strong husband? Without forming the words in her head, she suddenly knew what had happened.

Henrietta screamed his name over and over in cries and then moans. "Ben! Ben! Ben! Oh, my Ben! Where are you? Come back to me! Bennnn!"

Little Donnie, now abruptly awakened and terrified, took up the cries, too. "Unca Ben! Unca Ben!"

Daniel instantly understood what had happened and dove back into the water, blindly swimming back and forth between the two rafts. "Dad, Dad, Where Are You?" He yelled over and over every time he surfaced. Laura and the girls now began to scream for Ben, too. There was nothing more they could do.

It would truly have been a pitiful sight to see, if it had been possible to penetrate the early morning darkness. The only sounds now were the howl of the wind and the sound of the chilly, heaving water as it hit the rafts, then rolled over its victims. The vicious undertow beneath the dark waves, had now begun to suck up every bit of debris and the many victims in its path and, like a giant vacuum cleaner, was pulling them out to sea. As many people died from being trapped in the strong undertow as were drowned in the rising water and waves of the hurricane. So many had managed to cling to a floating object, but when the swift water grabbed their weakened limbs and jerked them downward, they lacked the strength to swim back to the top of the water and were helplessly pulled out to sea.

Daniel shouted words of comfort to Henrietta. "Ma, Pa is a great swimmer! He surely has caught hold of something to hang on to. He'll find us when the sun comes up. You'll see—don't worry about him!" Through his trembling words, he tried to convince her as well as himself that the unthinkable had not just happened. Ben would find them when it was light. The children calmed down as they listened to Daniel's words, but Laura and Henrietta both fell into silent shock. Now it was Dan's turn to pray, and pray he did, for his father's life to somehow be spared from the deadly undertow.

*****

Ben had helped Daniel tie the wet ropes onto the bushes as best they could, for they knew that this act would be all that would keep their rafts from being swept out to sea as the hurricane spent its fury. With ropes tied around their own waists, he and Daniel felt secure as they swam back to their rafts. But the ropes had become limp and stretched over hours in the seawater. Ben's rope was particularly slack and, as he was swimming back to the raft he, Henrietta and Donnie shared, a single huge wave swept over him. The rope suddenly slipped down the lower part of his body and was pulled off his legs and feet by the swift ebb tide.

In the waning darkness, Ben couldn't tell up from down as he held his breath and paddled frantically, but the strong undertow continued to sweep him away with it. Just as he was completely out of air, his hand touched something hard. In a last-second effort, Ben clutched it with both arms and kicked once more time. He shot upward and his head emerged from his watery prison, as he took in a much-needed breath of air. He hung onto the huge piece of debris, which was also caught in the swift undertow, and went whirling and churning up and down, around and around through the water, being propelled toward the sea. A few moments later, the debris slammed into something larger, firm and still. He felt a mighty blow land on his shoulder, its impact cracking a rib. Seeing the faces of his family flash before him, Ben renewed his grip on the piece of wood that had so far saved him.

Not accustomed to praying for himself, Benjamin Tilton found himself begging silently, *God, if only you will give me the strength to hold on, it will take more than this to separate me from them.* He suddenly realized that the wood he was holding on to was not moving because it had become ensnarled and was stuck fast within a larger object. He continued to hold on with every last bit of his strength until, finally, he felt the rush of the saltwater begin to slow a bit and a tiny streak of light appeared in the sky. *Thank you,* whispered the half-drowned man from his nest of debris in a small grove of mangled palm trees near the beach.

6:00AM~~By the Dawn's Early Light

The rain finally stopped and pale streaks of light shone in the eastern sky. As the morning dawned, it was still cloudy but they knew that the hurricane had finally passed over. The water kept receding in a powerful ebb tide. Soon, Daniel was the first to see that they were not stuck in bushes at all, but in a big, oak tree! All around them on the ground were piles of wreckage that had once been buildings and houses. Laura looked around and strained her eyes for signs of life but there was not a movement or a sound, nothing but silence. It seemed as though they were alone on a deserted island.

Cleaning Up After the Hurricane

"Look," Daniel called. "Over there!" He pointed to three buildings downtown still standing among the wreckage. The hull of the railroad station, the three-story bank, and courthouse had partially survived and the people who had taken shelter in them were alive.

The water level fell faster and faster as it drained back out into the sea. Daniel threw more rope around the tree trunks to hold them fast. Soon they could see the ground. Daniel cut the rope from around his waist and climbed down. Then he released Henrietta, Donnie, Laura and the girls. Slowly and stiffly, they descended from the big oak tree. Soon they were all standing in the mud hugging one another and crying with the sheer joy of being alive. Donnie clung to his mother as though he would never let go. Effie pulled me out of her apron, shook the water out of my torn clothes, and brushed dirt from my face, then kissed me and tucked me safely back inside her apron top.

Laura squinted her eyes in the weak light in a last effort to see Ben. Suddenly, she saw what seemed to be a disheveled old man limping toward them in the ankle-deep water. Could it be? Was it her brother? She stopped, drawing the attention of Henrietta and Daniel, who also looked in the direction she was pointing.

"Ben? Ben, is that you? Oh, Ben!" Henrietta cried out as she ran toward him and threw herself into his arms, as did all of the others. No more joyous reunion had even been held than that of this bedraggled little family on that muddy September morning.

The three-story courthouse was the closest building, so the family slowly made their way to it. They all trudged through the thick mud and the cold, deadly silence in their torn, soaked clothes, looking for all the world like beggars. The few people who passed by seemed to be aimlessly wandering while neither hearing nor seeing anyone. Effie's legs finally buckled beneath her, so Ben swept her up on his back and carried her. Next, Janie fell, so Daniel picked her up and carried her and the bruised procession straggled toward the shell of the nearest building.

That day was a very sad day for the people of Galveston. Over seven thousand people were missing! Almost every family on the island had lost loved ones. If it hadn't been for Ben's quick thinking, we would have been among the missing too. Our family stayed overnight in the courthouse, which was turned into a shelter. News traveled fast and soon boats with supplies began arriving from the mainland and volunteers came with food, water and blankets. Rachel, Henrietta, and Laura repeated over and over how blessed little Effie had been to hold on to me and not fall off the roof. Laura, of course, didn't mention that Effie said she heard me call to her. That would remain our very special secret.

Ben and Daniel set out to see if there was anything left of the house. Several hours later, they returned to tell the family that most of the houses were gone. They had found a large pile of yellow boards hung up in a grove of salt cedar trees not far from where the cement foundation still remained.

They had also found the schooner, *Black Jack II*, lying on its side and damaged but still intact, partly buried in the sand near the bay. All the docks and piers were completely gone and many of the boats tied there were grounded on the beach and ruined. The water had risen seventeen feet above sea level, washing away almost everything on the island and carrying it out to sea. Most of what was left was completely ruined.

Even though my family had lost everything, they knew that things could be repaired or replaced. I was glad that Effie had rescued me and that I had been able to help save her. And I didn't mind at all that I now had only one-half of my right leg!

Ben's brother, Dave, and many other men sailed across the bay from The Cove to help. They found the tattered family and rejoiced that they were all still alive. Then, they helped the family aboard Dave's boat and carried them all to Mother Annie's. The next day, the men returned to Galveston with food, first aid supplies, blankets and water, to begin helping the other survivors. Later, they were able to pull *Black Jack II* back into the harbor and tow the crippled schooner to The Cove. In time, they even helped Ben rebuild his home on the original foundation where it had stood and where Jean Lafitte's headquarters had stood eighty years before. Piers, bridges and railroad lines were also rebuilt and, the next year, the Tilton Hauling Business opened once again.

Henrietta grieved for the friends they had lost, especially Flossy and George MacClenny and their three children. Their good, Scottish neighbors had come to America in search of a better life, but it had slipped away from them during the night.

All evidence of the big Catholic Orphanage which had stood near the beach, with its devoted nuns and the ninety children they cared for, was also lost as though it had never stood there at all. The sisters, still holding their crosses and the orphans still clutched in their arms, were later found buried beneath the beach sand and debris. They had tied themselves to the children with ropes so they would not lose a single child.

Isaac Cline, the kindly weatherman, had sheltered over thirty people in his large, sturdy home. It had collapsed and washed away that dreadful night and his wife and children were swept out of his arms, leaving him all alone. He now walked about sadly and in shock searching for his family. His wife would later be found under fallen timber where she had drowned.

The brave people of Galveston grieved for their loved ones and friends; then they did what brave people do. They started over. Heavy equipment was brought in to the island by boat and used to pump sand in from the Gulf to raise the entire island. Then the people began to build a long, fifteen-foot-high, concrete seawall to hopefully keep the ocean from ever flooding their town again. This had been the deadliest natural disaster in North American history and the survivors were determined that never again would so many people lose their lives to a Galveston hurricane. Some people left the island to begin their lives again on the mainland, but many, determined people, like Ben, Henrietta, and Dan, remained and began to put their city and their lives back together again.

Once back at our home in The Cove, Laura made me a new blue, gingham dress and kissed me as she placed me up on my shelf in the parlor. She knew that Effie would have slipped off the roof on that terrible night if she had not held on to me. "Is it really possible," whispered Laura softly, "that you called to my little Effie and told her to hold on to you? If you did, I want to thank you, Annabelle. Perhaps God sent you to us to protect our darling Effie that awful night. You are our heroine and our little angel and I will always love you."

Big tears of gratitude filled her eyes and spilled over onto her cheeks. She was a resolute, frontier woman like her staunch, pioneering mother and grandmother and hardly ever cried. But now she sank down on the sofa and, holding me tightly, rocked back and forth for a long time, heaving deep sobs of relief and uttering prayers of thanks. Her tears splashed down onto my dress but I didn't mind at all because I loved my Laura.

Afterward, with a smile of assurance, she dried her eyes with the corner of her apron, and placed me back on my shelf. Then she picked up her broom and, humming a little tune, finished her sweeping. This is the kind of pioneer strength and courage that runs in my, and most other, enduring Texas families. When troubles arise, they face them squarely with staunch faith and steadfastness, and, afterward, set their faces toward the future.

* * * * *

Dear Reader:

Effie and I had a very special bond after the hurricane, although I never said anything to her again. At night she would lie in bed and talk to me because she knew I could understand her. Of course, Effie, like her mother, grew up and I sat on a shelf once more, until she gave me to her little daughter, Charlene, which is another story, but now I was content. I knew that life would go on and changes would be all right. I understood that, in time, there would always be another little girl and new owner to love me and there was.

I am loved in spite of my missing leg because each mother tells her daughters my story. They call it my badge of courage, although, to me, it was simply a gift of love. I am so glad that Frau Anjabel made me different. Being unique is a good thing. Sure enough, I have now been handed down, now to a fifth generation daughter in our big family. Since Effie was my owner, I've had many more adventures through the years and hope to have many more. Perhaps someday, I will tell you about them.

I have learned to love and cherish the time I spend with each little girl who owns me in each new generation of my wonderful Texas family and realize that I am very blessed to be a part of it. I am so glad that Ben and Dan Tilton chose me from that crate of dolls on Galveston beach so long ago. I am now almost a hundred and fifty years old and often wonder what adventures the next hundred years holds for me. Who knows? I may even speak to another little girl someday!

Always your friend, Annabelle

Our Heirloom Porcelain Doll, (Made in Germany, 1871) Annabelle

Great-Grandmother Laura Tilton's Original "Tea Cake" Recipe
(Big Sugar Cookies)

Start early in the cool of the day. Stoke up a good medium fire in wood stove.

Mix: 1 pound of fresh churned butter or fresh rendered hog lard
    2 pounds of sugar
    4 Tablespoons of vanilla
Stir well in a big bowl.

Add: 6 fresh eggs, preferably fresh-gathered this morning and mix together.

Then: 4 pounds of flour
    ½ cup of baking powder
    2 pinches of cinnamon if you have it
    1 Tablespoon salt

Finally Add: 1 cup of fresh sweet milk (a little more if dough is too tough)
    2-3 cups of pecans or other nuts if you have them

Mix all of this well, using a large wooden spoon and your biggest bowl.

Divide dough into 3 parts. With a rolling pin, roll out 1 part on clean, floured board to ½ inch thick. Put the other 2 parts in the icebox until you are ready for them.

Cut cookies with a canning jar lid to make a big 3inch cookie.

Put cookies on cookie sheet and sprinkle them with sugar.
Cook on the oven shelf for 15 minutes, checking often and adding wood as needed.
Keep on till all the dough has been made into 12 dozen big cookies for family.

Boil water, go out and pick several sprigs of mint or get out some sassafras shavings,

and brew yourself a cup of mint or sassafras tea. Go sit down on the porch. Drink tea

and eat some cookies to relax before starting supper.

This family recipe has been handed down from Annie Tilton to her daughter, Laura, to

her daughter, Effie, to her daughter Charlene, to her daughters, Susan and Evelyn, to their

daughters, Kristi and Suzanne, and finally to their daughters, Jaci, Cassie and Katie.